Concise. Accessible. Beautifully written. Christa's book is a gift to our church as it reminds us of the gift that is *the* Church. All members should have this on their shelves and return to it when they feel tempted to skip out of any gathering of God's people. Christa delivers her book at a perfect time, when now, more than ever, the Christian has the opportunity to choose virtual services over attending corporal worship and communal reception of the Word. Christa encourages us to meet together, echoing the author of Hebrews, and reveals why we would never want to give up the precious gift of being gathered by Christ.

—STEPHANIE NEUGEBAUER, MA, CONCORDIA SEMINARY, ST. LOUIS; PASTOR'S WIFE AND MOTHER

Petzold gets right at the heart of what it means to be the Body of Christ, skillfully weaving together a case for Christian ecclesiology that uses the tools of theology, history, and a keen observation of our current cultural condition. This text can serve as a bedrock description of the Church's origins and scriptural foundations, but it also presses the reader toward the ultimate telos for which the Church strives. Unflinchingly committed to *sola Scriptura* and *solus Christus*, this book will be a blessing to many.

—DR. JOEL OESCH, PROFESSOR OF THEOLOGY AT CONCORDIA UNIVERSITY IRVINE, AUTHOR OF *CROSSING WIRES: MAKING SENSE OF TECHNOLOGY, TRANSHUMANISM, AND CHRISTIAN IDENTITY*

Gathered by Christ beautifully combines Scripture and Church history to paint a picture of God's design for His Bride, the struggles the Church has faced throughout history, and how these form our view of and our responsibility as the Church today. While acknowledging the pain that sin has caused in churches, Christa Petzold points us back to the Church as a beautiful gift of God through which He continually points us to Christ! In a culture focused on individuality and conflict avoidance, *Gathered by Christ* is an excellent reminder of the community we have in Christ, seeking *sincere* unity in the Church.

—Tara Darling, director of Christian education,
St. Paul Lutheran Church, Mount Vernon, Iowa

In the midst of deep doubts and confusing misunderstandings about the Church in our increasingly unchurched society comes this delightful, well-written, and incredibly helpful book from a mother, a pastor's wife, and an astute theologian. Christa Petzold reminds us that the Church is far more than an organized association, a Sunday breakfast club, or even a helpful support group. Insightfully grounded in Scripture, informed by ample references to Church history, and illustrated by practical examples, Petzold's book leads the reader to see the Church from Jesus' perspective as the Body of Christ—the very family of God. The reader comes away with a renewed sense of awe, excitement, and hope in being part of this often-overlooked gift we call Church.

—Rev. Dr. Glenn K. Fluegge, director of the
Cross-cultural Ministry Center and professor of
theology at Concordia University Irvine

Gathered by Christ

The Overlooked Gift of Church

CHRISTA PETZOLD

CONCORDIA PUBLISHING HOUSE · SAINT LOUIS

To my parents, Robert and Susan Lindstrom

Thank you for raising me in a family where church was a given, not an option.

Published by Concordia Publishing House
3558 S. Jefferson Avenue, St. Louis, MO 63118-3968
1-800-325-3040 • cph.org

1 2 3 4 5 6 7 8 9 10   32 31 30 29 28 27 26 25 24 23

Contents

Preface

. . . .

What is the Church? What role does the Church play in the lives of her members? For many today, the answers to these questions are not obvious. We no longer live in a world that assumes that being a Christian means participating in the life of the Church. This book aims to provide a biblical study of what the Church is and show why the Church is a necessity and a blessing in the lives of the faithful and in the world.

In a book about what it means to be the Church, it feels natural to include references to Church history. To this end, each chapter starts with a vignette that highlights a writing, Church Father, or theologian from a past era in Church history. The vignettes are presented in chronological order (with one exception) and provide a quotation and basic background information on the individual highlighted.

I included these vignettes for several reasons: First, these Church Fathers have valuable insights that are applicable to our context. Second, they serve as a reminder that the issues we face in the Church today are not new; we can learn from the Church's rich history of addressing such challenges. And finally, Church history is our family history as God's people. It is a beautiful thing to get to know those who have gone before us and who are part of our story. Numerous individuals and writings could have been highlighted, but I chose examples that seemed to fit with the content of this book. Nothing should be inferred from which Church Fathers are included or not included. Each chapter stands alone without the initial vignette, so if any specific quotation is difficult to follow, the reader can skip it without significantly affecting the flow.

Because one's own theological convictions will inevitably show through when writing about this topic, it is helpful for readers to be aware of an author's bias up front. Therefore, I will state plainly that I write from the perspective of confessional Lutheranism. Out of a desire to provide something explicit and helpful, I have not shied away from pointing out the differences in how various theological traditions see the Church. Still, I love and respect my brothers and sisters in Christ in other traditions. As this study grounds itself in Scripture, I believe the message of the Church as a gift from Christ to His people will shine through and be encouraging to readers, regardless of their background.

Introduction

·····································

As the bridegroom rejoices over the bride,
so shall your God rejoice over you.

Have you ever heard someone say, "I like Jesus, but I'm not so sure about the Church"? Perhaps you have felt this way yourself. Maybe you know people who say they believe in Jesus and His death and resurrection but do not participate in a church community.

Sometimes people reject the Church because they've been hurt. Like all gatherings of humans, churches are full of sinners who fail to live up to God's standards and cause pain for others. People who grew up in church may stop attending because they no longer believe their church's teachings or because they fail to see the connection between those teachings and what happens on Sunday mornings. Still others are discouraged and confused by institutional divisions and denominations, feeling that something so fragmented with so much internal conflict cannot be trusted to provide answers to life's biggest questions.

Such concerns are understandable. Sin, division, confusion, false teaching, and hypocrisy—seeing these in the Church is enough to make anyone want to walk away. This may be how our experiences have led us to see the Church, but how does Jesus see her? While we see the Church as divided, hopelessly fragmented by theological differences and cultural barriers, Scripture tells us that Jesus sees her as one, holy, and unified in Him. We see the Church as full of sinners, but Jesus sees her as a communion of saints washed by His blood and made pure and blameless. We see the Church as existentially threatened by an increasingly secular world, but Jesus sees her as faithful and triumphant in Him, a colony of the new creation that is promised with certainty. We see the Church as defined by what we do as church members, while Jesus sees her as defined by what He has already done.

I am blessed to be married to a pastor, so I have a front-row seat both to the beauty and joy of the Church at her best and to the challenges and heartbreak of the Church at her worst. My husband and I were at seminary when we had our first child, and I remember memorizing "The Church's One Foundation," one of my favorite hymns, with the intention of singing it to her every night as I put her to sleep. Here is the first stanza:

> **The Church's one foundation**
> **Is Jesus Christ, her Lord;**
> **She is His new creation**
> **By water and the Word.**
> **From heav'n He came and sought her**
> **To be His holy bride;**
> **With His own blood He bought her,**
> **And for her life He died. (*LSB* 644:1)**

One day my mom asked why I chose that particular hymn. I told her that I knew my kids were also going to have a front-row seat to the Church's strengths and struggles. I wanted to imprint upon their hearts and minds that the Church is something beautiful, something founded securely on Jesus Christ, and something objectively rooted in God's Word—not in the sinful words and actions of the individuals who make up our church communities.

When I hear people say, "I like Jesus but not the Church," it drives me to empathy. What pain and life experiences hide beneath such a statement? But I also find myself pondering how Jesus would respond. The Bible describes the Church as the Bride of Christ. If "From heav'n He came and sought her To be His holy bride; With His own blood He bought her, And for her life He died," as the hymn puts it, would Jesus appreciate such a negative sentiment? Saying you like Jesus but not His Church seems akin to saying, "You're welcome here, Jesus, but You can't bring Your wife."

Sometimes in Scripture, Jesus responded harshly to "church" leaders. But He never disparages the Church itself. In Matthew 23, Jesus rebuked the Pharisees for oppressing God's people through self-righteous attitudes and legalism. Yet even in His righteous anger against the religious leaders, Jesus did not undermine their authority. He said, "The scribes and the Pharisees sit on Moses' seat, so do and observe whatever they tell you, but not the works they do. For they preach, but do not practice" (Matthew 23:2–3). "Moses' seat" refers to the Scriptures, the Word of God as given to Moses (specifically, the first five books of the Old Testament). Jesus upheld the authority God gives to His Church through Scripture, even as He condemned those specific religious leaders. The oppressive and hard-hearted Pharisees were the problem, not religion itself.

As we get to know the Church through Jesus' eyes, we will meet Christians from other eras and places. The Church is timeless—a community made up of the faithful throughout the world and those who are now in heaven with Jesus. The final stanza of "The Church's One Foundation" captures this timelessness:

> **Yet she on earth has union**
> **With God, the Three in One,**
> **And mystic sweet communion**
> **With those whose rest is won.**
> **O blessèd heav'nly chorus!**
> **Lord, save us by Your grace**
> **That we, like saints before us,**
> **May see You face to face.** (*LSB* 644:5)

When we face challenges as Christians, we can take comfort in this legacy of faith: For two thousand years, Christians have encountered struggles of every kind and yet have stood firm on the Word of God. The Holy Spirit has been working through this communion of saints to build up the Church since Pentecost. May the stories and writings of some of those saints at rest, found in the vignettes at the start of each chapter, encourage us as we learn more about how Jesus sees the Church.

I pray this book leads you to reflect not only on what Jesus has done for you as an individual but also on how Jesus' atoning work crafts us into something new: the Body of Christ. May we learn to see the Bride of Christ through the eyes of her Bridegroom and, in doing so, draw comfort from the knowledge that we are part of the Church, this timeless community of faith rooted in Jesus Christ, her Lord.

PART I

How Jesus Sees the Church

· ·

What the Church *Is*

*T*ertullian was a theologian who lived in Africa about two hundred years after Jesus. In his writing, *The Apology,* he describes what Christians do when they gather together:

> We are a body knit together as such by a common religious profession, by unity of discipline, and by the bond of a common hope. We meet together as an assembly and congregation, that, offering up prayer to God as with united force, we may wrestle with Him in our supplications. . . . We pray, too, for the emperors, for their ministers and for all in authority, for the welfare of the world, for the prevalence of peace, for the delay of the final consummation. We assemble to read our sacred writings, if any peculiarity of the times makes either forewarning or reminiscence needful. However it be in that respect, with the sacred words we nourish our faith, we animate our hope, we make our confidence more steadfast.[1]

---

1   Tertullian, *The Apology* XXXIX, in *Latin Christianity: Its Founder, Tertullian,* ed. Alexander Roberts, James

I find this description a beautiful and encouraging picture of Christian community. We also see in this description three specific elements of the Church. These three elements will guide the structure of this book and help us answer the question "What makes the Church *the Church*?" There is a religious profession—the content of our faith. There is a manner of living—the unity of discipline, or the habits of the Christian, such as gathering together weekly around the Word and Sacraments. And there is a specific hope that we all share—the belief that Jesus Christ, who died and rose for our salvation, will come back again "with glory to judge both the living and the dead, whose kingdom will have no end" (Nicene Creed).

How do these three elements define the Church? It all starts with Jesus. He is the Creator, Redeemer, and Sustainer of the Church, and we will explore what that means in part I of this book.

Donaldson, and A. Cleveland Coxe, The Ante-Nicene Fathers, vol. 3 (Buffalo, NY: The Christian Literature Company, 1885), 46. Spelling has been modernized for clarity.

The Origin of the Church

··

THE DIDACHE

The Didache is an ancient Christian text. While the exact dates are not known, it was written either before or around AD 150, only a few generations after the New Testament books were written. Unlike Scripture, the Didache is not infallible. If you read it in full, you'd likely disagree with some parts or see things that differ from what your pastor teaches. In every era, theologians write about the life of the Church and theology and practice, and just as in our own day, some writings are more theologically sound than others.

Still, the essentials of Christianity have stayed the same throughout the history of the Church. Reading the Didache and other writings like it reminds us of this truth. We also benefit from seeing our faith through the eyes of Christians who lived in an entirely different time and place. Our lives, culture, and assumptions about the world radically differ from those of the first generations of Christians. Yet despite these differences, we see much continuity in the practices and life of the Church.

Knowing we are part of this rich history provides comfort and a sense of security in our faith.

The Greek word *didache* (pronounced dih-dah-KAY) means "the teaching." The writing is short, the length of an article rather than a book, and it is sometimes called "The Teachings of the Twelve Apostles." It begins with a section on keeping the Law, in which the "two ways" are contrasted—the way of life and the way of death—and expounds on the two greatest commandments: love God and love neighbor. Next, it describes church practices, covering Baptism, the Eucharist, worshiping on Sunday morning each week, electing bishops and deacons for service in the church, fasting and prayer life, and so on. It ends with a call to watch for Jesus' return.

This excerpt from the Didache discusses worship and the life of the Church:

> **And concerning baptism, thus baptize ye: Having first said all these things, baptize into the name of the Father, and of the Son, and of the Holy Spirit, in living water. But if thou have not living water, baptize into other water; and if thou canst not in cold, in warm. But if thou have not either, pour out water thrice upon the head into the name of Father and Son and Holy Spirit. . . .**
>
> **Now concerning the Thanksgiving (Eucharist), thus give thanks. First, concerning the cup: We thank thee, our Father, for the holy vine of David Thy servant, which Thou madest known to us through Jesus Thy Servant; to Thee be the glory for ever. And concerning the broken bread: We thank Thee, our Father, for the life and knowledge which Thou madest known to us through Jesus Thy Servant; to Thee be the glory for ever. Even as this broken bread was scattered over the hills, and was gathered together and became one,**

so let Thy Church be gathered together from the ends of the earth into Thy kingdom; for Thine is the glory and the power through Jesus Christ forever. But let no one eat or drink of your Thanksgiving (Eucharist), but they who have been baptized into the name of the Lord; for concerning this also the Lord hath said, Give not that which is holy to the dogs. . . .

Whosoever, therefore, cometh and teacheth you all these things that have been said before, receive him. But if the teacher himself turn and teach another doctrine to the destruction of this, hear him not; but if he teach so as to increase righteousness and the knowledge of the Lord, receive him as the Lord. . . .

Appoint, therefore, for yourselves, bishops and deacons worthy of the Lord, men meek, and not lovers of money, and truthful and proved; for they also render to you the service of prophets and teachers.[2]

Despite the cumbersome translation, we can easily recognize the Word preached and Sacraments observed in the first century after Jesus' death. We see practices such as Baptism (either by pouring water or by immersion), only communing baptized members in good standing, and vigilance about the purity of doctrine to be taught within the Church. Readings like this help us see how much of church life has remained constant throughout time and across cultures. This points us to a comforting truth: God is the one who preserves and sustains His Church.

---

2 Selections from Didache 7–15, in *Fathers of the Third and Fourth Centuries,* ed. Alexander Roberts, James Donaldson, and A. Cleveland Coxe, The Ante-Nicene Fathers, vol. 7 (Buffalo, NY: Christian Literature Company, 1886), 379–81.

God Calls His People

. . . .

From the backstories of our favorite fictional characters to the draw of movie prequels to the joy of swapping life stories with a new friend—who doesn't love a good origin story? We all see the value in knowing how we got to where we are. To understand someone or something, we must go back to the beginning and ask, "How did this all start?"

Understanding the origin of the Church is no different. Was the Church created by religious leaders a few hundred years after Christ? Was it created by popes, councils, or bureaucrats? Did Jesus mean to found a religious movement? These are important questions, and people have answered them in various ways. Scripture provides the true origin story of the Church: a community of faith gathered by God and called to be His people since the beginning of time. This is what the historic Christian Church believes about herself.

Why does Scripture dictate what the Church believes? Because Jesus says so. The Christian Church revolves around one person: Jesus of Nazareth. Jesus was a real person who lived and was crucified by the Roman authorities around AD 30; this is not disputed even by unbelievers.

In many New Testament passages, Jesus assumes the authority of Scripture. One such passage is Matthew 5:17–18: "Do not think that I have come to abolish the Law or the Prophets; I have not come to abolish them but to fulfill them. For truly, I say to you, until heaven and earth pass away, not an iota, not a dot, will pass from the Law until all is accomplished." The phrase "the Law and the Prophets" refers to the books of the Old Testament. "The Law" was shorthand for the first five books, written by Moses; "the Prophets" encompassed the other Old Testament authors.

We have eyewitness accounts of many people seeing Him alive after His crucifixion, and it is a fact that His disciples were transformed within the span of a month from men hiding and afraid in a locked room to men willing to be killed for the sake of their testimony that Jesus was truly God and had risen from the dead. Since the time of Jesus' resurrection, the Church has consisted of people who profess the truth that Jesus is God, that He died to atone for the sins of the world, that He rose from the dead in the flesh, and that He will come back again and His kingdom will have no end. Jesus considers Scripture to be authoritative. Therefore, Scripture's testimony is central to our understanding of God and of ourselves.

The Church's origin story is embedded in the world's origin story. The first chapters of Genesis tell of God creating and calling His people. When God created Adam and Eve, He designed them to be in community with Himself and with each other. By giving them the command not to eat from the tree of the knowledge of good and evil, God gave them a way to worship Him. With this one command, God introduced Adam and Eve to His Law: the reality that He was God and they were not.

But instead of keeping His Law, Adam and Eve disobeyed God and ate the fruit, destroying the communal relationship between mankind and God. But God reacted with compassion. He promised Adam and Eve right there in the garden, with the bitterness of the first sin still hanging in the air, that He would fix this (see Genesis 3:15). From that moment, Scripture tells the story of God calling His people out of a fallen world, making them His own, and dwelling among them while working throughout history to restore what was broken and make all things new.

The theme of God calling His people and making them holy echoes throughout the Bible. Before the great flood (see Genesis 6–8), God called Noah to build an ark of protection from the judgment that would be sent on the earth. God Himself shut Noah and his family in the ark (see Genesis 7:16). He was the one acting to call Noah out from among the sinful people of the world, saving Noah and his family from death.

In Genesis 15, God established a covenant with Abraham to make him into a great people and to give him a land to possess:

> And He brought him outside and said, "Look toward heaven, and number the stars, if you are able to number them." Then He said to him, "So shall your offspring be." And he believed the LORD, and He counted it to him as righteousness. And He said to him, "I am the LORD who brought you out from Ur of the Chaldeans to give you this land to possess." (vv. 5–7)

The promise God made to Abraham had two components: offspring that cannot be counted (a great people) and a land to dwell in and possess. Abraham did only one thing as his part of the covenant—he believed the Lord, and God counted that as righteousness. All that Abraham contributed to the relationship was believing the Word of God, and that is exactly how God wanted it.

Abraham eventually tried to help God bring about the promised blessings by having a child with his wife's servant, Hagar. But this was not God's desire or plan. Rather, Abraham was in God's grace when he passively received the promises, trusting God to create and call His people. Despite Abraham's mistaken attempts to seize control, God still kept His covenant with Abraham.

Hundreds of years later, God delivered Abraham's descendants out of slavery in Egypt, giving them His Law and renewing His call to be His people. He continued to promise that they would be His people and have a land of their own.

God's promises are tangible and always involve Him creating a community and planting that community in a promised land. From Adam and Eve, who were in fellowship with God in a garden, to Noah and his family stepping off the ark onto dry land to the Israelites entering the Promised Land, God approaches His people collectively and benevolently, always.

A House for David

. . . .

We tend to think of church as what we do for God. In reality, the Church is what God does for us. King David learned this lesson in 2 Samuel 7 when God made a covenant with him. This is yet another instance of God establishing His people through His own strength, design, and plan. David presided over God's people during a time of peace and prosperity in the Promised Land. As David looked around at the blessings God had granted him, he was moved to do something for God in return:

> Now when [King David] lived in his house and the
> LORD had given him rest from all his surrounding
> enemies, the king said to Nathan the prophet, "See
> now, I dwell in a house of cedar, but the ark of God
> dwells in a tent." And Nathan said to the king, "Go,
> do all that is in your heart, for the LORD is with you."
> (2 Samuel 7:1–3)

In the very first line, we read that God was the one who gave David rest from his enemies. David does not get the credit; God's people residing peacefully in the Promised Land was a gift from God. David wanted to repay God, to bring glory to God's name, by building Him a temple. This seems like a noble goal, but God had different plans.

In the next verses of this chapter, God sent the prophet Nathan to remind David of all that He had done in David's life. God is the one who took David from the pasture, made him king, defeated David's enemies, and used David's rule to appoint a place for His people, Israel. God also reminded David that in all the days since He delivered Israel from slavery in Egypt, He had never demanded a house of cedar. God desired to be worshiped not according to David's plans but according to His Word and instruction.

God went on to promise David even more blessings. While David had desired to build a house for God, God turned the tables and insisted He would build a house for David:

> The LORD declares to you that *the Lord will make you a house*. When your days are fulfilled and you lie down with your fathers, I will raise up your offspring after you, who shall come from your body, and I will establish His kingdom. He shall build a house for My name, and I will establish the throne of His kingdom forever.
> . . . And your house and your kingdom shall be made sure forever before Me. Your throne shall be established forever. (2 Samuel 7:11–13, 16, emphasis added)

God fulfilled His promise in two ways: first through the reign and legacy of Solomon, David's son, and ultimately through the promised Messiah. The throne that will be established forever is Jesus' throne. God did allow Solomon, David's son, to build a temple for Him, but David learned here that God is the one who establishes His people. He establishes their house, not the other way around. David, feeling good about himself, resolved to build something for God, and God turned it around and taught David that this is not the way it works. We can do nothing for God. He builds everything for us.

In this account from David's life, we learn with David that our relationship with God is based not on what we do for Him but on what He does for us. The Church is the community that God Himself physically gathers together, calls out from the peoples of the world, and establishes into an eternal kingdom. This is the kingdom of God that Jesus teaches about throughout the Gospels. As God taught

David, the Church is not created, sustained, or built up by man. God does all the work. God alone creates, calls, and gathers His people; God alone teaches them and makes them holy. Human pride often causes us to overlook this simple truth: God builds the Church.

The Head of the Church

G od's promise to David to establish his house forever found its ultimate fulfillment in the Messiah. Through the life, death, and resurrection of Jesus, we are made into this long-awaited community—the Body of Christ. Paul's Epistle to the Colossians says this about Jesus' fulfillment of the Old Testament promises:

> He is the image of the invisible God, the firstborn of all
> creation. For by Him all things were created, in heaven
> and on earth, visible and invisible, whether thrones or
> dominions or rulers or authorities—all things were
> created through Him and for Him. And He is before
> all things, and in Him all things hold together. And
> He is the head of the body, the church. He is the begin-
> ning, the firstborn from the dead, that in everything He
> might be preeminent. For in Him all the fullness of God
> was pleased to dwell, and through Him to reconcile
> to Himself all things, whether on earth or in heaven,
> making peace by the blood of His cross. (1:15–20)

In this text, Paul records an ancient hymn that articulates the relationship between Jesus and the Church. The structure of these verses suggests it was used liturgically in a church setting. The hymn may already have been in use in Colossae when Paul wrote this letter, or Paul may have been the author. The composition suggests it was written by someone with exegetical and liturgical training.[3]

---

3   Paul E. Deterding, *Colossians*, Concordia Commentary (St. Louis: Concordia Publishing House, 2003), 43.

This hymn beautifully professes the faith of the Early Church and demonstrates the link between their faith and their worship. These verses affirm that Jesus is the Head of the Church, and they also model what church hymns should do: proclaim the truth of Jesus Christ.

The hymn declares that Jesus "is the image of the invisible God" (v. 15). To image something is to represent it completely and perfectly. Because Jesus is "of one substance with the Father" (Nicene Creed), we encounter God Himself in the person of Jesus Christ. The mystery and beauty of the incarnation is that through Jesus, God comes to us physically, tangibly, and bodily. Jesus, the Second Person of the Trinity, is the one we encounter with our flesh. He is also "the firstborn of all creation. . . . By Him all things were created" (vv. 15–16). Everything that exists owes its creation and continued existence and thriving to Jesus. These verses profess a faith in Jesus as the one who makes every aspect of our lives meaningful in every way. He is central to all reality. That is what is meant by "that in everything He might be preeminent" (v. 18).

Read Colossians 1:15–20 again slowly. Notice how the hymn acclaims Christ as our Creator, Sustainer, Savior, and Reconciler. He was there at the beginning, He was there for our redemption, He will be there at the end. And at the center of this hymnic, credal passage, we read, "He is the head of the body, the church" (v. 18). In his commentary on Colossians, Paul Deterding writes:

> Although Christ is the head over the entire creation . . . , only the church is called his body, and Christ as the head is connected to the church as his body. Therefore, the apostle's designation of the church as the body of which Christ is the head indicates that the church stands in a unique relationship to the one who is head over all things. This unique relationship is one of salvation, for it is a result of Christ's redemptive work. . . . Paul uses this terminology of head and body

to emphasize the oneness of the church, a unity which already exists as a gift of grace and which cannot be created by any effort on the part of believers.[4]

Jesus rules over all of creation, and everything exists in Him according to His mercy and will. And yet, the relationship between Jesus and the Church is much more intimate than the relationship between Jesus and all creation. The oneness that the Church has in Christ is not metaphorical. It is given to us in real, tangible ways. Just as God called out His people in the Old Testament and promised them a physical place to be united in Him, so also Jesus' Church is united in Him and given His true and real presence in the Sacrament of the Lord's Supper. God has promised complete reconciliation, that all things will be made new, beautiful, and perfect when Jesus returns. But while we wait for that day, we are not alone or cut off from our Lord. Jesus has left us physical connections to His forgiveness and mercy in the Sacraments. The relationship that each member of the Church has with her Head, Jesus, and with one another is created in Baptism and sustained in the Lord's Supper. As the Head, Jesus creates the Church, sustains the Church, saves the Church, and will reconcile all things to Himself through His Body, the Church.

The next verses in Colossians continue:

> And you, who once were alienated and hostile in mind, doing evil deeds, He has now reconciled in His body of flesh by His death, in order to present you holy and blameless and above reproach before Him, if indeed you continue in the faith, stable and steadfast, not shifting from the hope of the gospel that you heard, which has been proclaimed in all creation under heaven, and of which I, Paul, became a minister. (1:21–23)

---

4   Deterding, *Colossians*, 58.

At this point, Paul makes it personal. He tells us where we fit into the story of who Jesus is and what Jesus has done. Our condition before encountering Jesus was "alienated and hostile in mind, doing evil deeds" (v. 21), but this is what it means to be the Church: we are now "reconciled in His body of flesh by His death" (v. 22). Just as God called His people out of slavery in Egypt, He now calls us out of our slavery to sin. As His holy and blameless people, we are above reproach if we continue in this faith and hold on to the hope we have received. This is the Church!

In this passage, the original Greek text makes clear the collective nature of the Church. The Greek language has different words for *you* singular and *you* plural. In English, we have only the one word *you*; we rely on context to determine whether a text addresses a single person or a group. In Colossians 1, Paul uses *you* plural. We may read the New Testament and assume the writers are speaking to their audiences personally in an individualistic way, but that would be a mistranslation and would fail to recognize the communal nature of the epistles. It isn't "And you, Christa, who once was alienated . . . , He has now reconciled." It's "And *you all*, Christians of Colossae, who once were alienated . . . , He has now reconciled in His body of flesh by His death, in order to present *you all* holy and blameless," and so on. This passage shows that we are all reconciled to Christ together as a body—as *His* Body.

This translation challenge is not unique to Colossians 1. Many of the New Testament Epistles are addressed to entire congregations. When we read the whole letter, including the introduction and the salutation at the end, the group nature is obvious, but we can miss this context when we read only a few verses at a time. We learn more about the nature of the Church when we realize these verses speak not only to us as individuals but also to the Church as a whole.

Comfort in Community

. . . .

T he Church as God's collective people is an inescapable reality in Scripture. Our twenty-first-century American way of talking about the Christian life tends to emphasize our own inner world. It focuses on "my personal relationship with Jesus" or "my individual faith walk" or "my unique journey." Sometimes this emphasis produces "go-it-alone" Christians, believers who don't think regular church involvement is necessary. Of course, the faith of the individual believer is a theme in Scripture, and each person will stand alone before God on the final day. But these two things—individual faith and a collective people—always go together.

We read this explicitly in Paul's Letter to the Corinthians:

> For just as the body is one and has many members,
> and all the members of the body, though many, are
> one body, so it is with Christ. For in one Spirit we were
> all baptized into one body—Jews or Greeks, slaves or
> free—and all were made to drink of one Spirit. For
> the body does not consist of one member but of many.
> (1 Corinthians 12:12–14)

Through Baptism, we become members of this Body, the Church—individual parts but united in one whole. The reality is inescapable: all Christians are members of the Church, whether or not they value this membership.

Human families provide another picture of this. When babies are born, they have no say about which family they are born into. Even when children grow up apart from their birth family, the reality of their birth is always a part of who they are. In the same way, we are born into the family of God through the waters of Baptism, and we can't escape that communal aspect.

The Church, the family of God, exists as Jesus' way of tangibly caring for each of us before His return. We were made for community, we long for community, and our God provides for us by placing us in community through His institutions of marriage, family, the Church, and the state. In Scripture, we see that these institutions are created, sanctioned, and blessed by God to image different aspects of His care and love to His people. Because of sin, sometimes those with God-given authority cannot be trusted. We may struggle with mistrust of institutions and hierarchy because of our life experiences. But that does not mean the institution they represent is bad in and of itself. Our God has all of creation under His control at all times, and He has given us the Church as a gift, a beautiful creation instituted by Jesus to bless and care for us. This institution should bring the Christian comfort, peace, and hope.

In the Large Catechism, Martin Luther describes the way the Church provides comfort to us:

> Everything, therefore, in the Christian Church is ordered toward this goal: we shall daily receive in the Church nothing but the forgiveness of sin through the Word and signs, to comfort and encourage our consciences as long as we live here. So even though we have sins, the grace of the Holy Spirit does not allow them to harm us. For we are in the Christian Church, where there is nothing but continuous, uninterrupted forgiveness of sin. This is because God forgives us and because we forgive, bear with, and help one another [Galatians 6:1–2].[5]

Luther understood that the Church is the means through which God delivers His forgiveness and salvation to each of us individually. Through that forgiveness, we are brought into the Church, and

---

5   Large Catechism II 55.

together we comprise the Body of Christ. The institutional Church is this Body. When people encounter the Church, they should also encounter God's promise of forgiveness and salvation in Christ. This is why Luther felt it was important to stand up for the Word of God when the church of his day was neglecting to offer that forgiveness (we will explore this in more depth later).

Luther continues: "But outside of this Christian Church, where the Gospel is not found, there is no forgiveness, as also there can be no holiness. Therefore, all who seek and wish to earn holiness not through the Gospel and forgiveness of sin, but by their works, have expelled and severed themselves from this Church [Galatians 5:4]."[6]

Luther was speaking specifically about the Roman Church of his day—their emphasis on works righteousness and their failure to preach the Gospel—but his insight can also be applied to those who don't participate in the life of the Church today. We may try to justify this neglect of Christ's Church with sentiments like, "I read my Bible and pray and try to be a good person. I don't need the Church to be saved." Trusting in our own ability to find a pleasing spiritual life for ourselves is exactly what Luther was talking about; it's trusting in our own works instead of humbly receiving the gift of forgiveness through the Church as instituted by Christ.

The point of this chapter is not to condemn anyone who has had negative or neglectful thoughts about church but to help us see the Church through Jesus' eyes. If you have ever thought something like this about your own spiritual life, know that you are not alone. Our culture overemphasizes individual spirituality and immerses us in a sea of confusing and unbiblical teachings. In this challenging context, we can easily be swept away by false doctrine. We desire to learn more about this Church that Jesus has created through His Word and by His forgiveness to comfort us and strengthen our faith. The rest of this book will explore how the Church provides

---

6   Large Catechism II 56.

these things for us in a concrete way, with Scripture and the faithful witnesses of those who have gone before us as our guide.

In the introduction to this section, we read Tertullian's summary of the Church as having three components: "a common religious profession," "unity of discipline," and "the bond of a common hope." We could state this succinctly as *creed, practice,* and *eschatological hope.* This chapter explored how the Church is instituted by Christ. Each of these elements of what it means to be the Church is grounded in the identity of our Savior. *Creed* is what we believe about who Jesus is and what He has done, *practice* is how Jesus interacts with us today, and the *eschatological hope* is what we expect and believe that Jesus will do in the future.

> *Eschatology* means "study of the end times." Our eschatological hope is our hope in what is to come when Christ returns.

Each of the next three chapters examines one component of Christian community more closely. In chapter 2, we will consider the creed or rule of faith—the role our teaching and profession of faith has in the Church and the way this specific set of teachings is central to the Church's identity. In chapter 3, we will consider the practices of the Church. This "unity of discipline" that Tertullian mentions refers to anything that Christians always do when they gather together as the Church. In chapter 4, we will talk about our "hope of the life to come" and how it shapes the Church's identity in the present.

Final Thought

• • • • • • • • • • • •

The Church is built not by man but by God, and Jesus is the Head of the Church. Because God is the one who brings each of His children into His Church, every Christian is part of the family of God. Whether or not we cherish this family and draw comfort from our role in it, we are a part of it. Through Christ, we are knit together as one Body, made holy on account of His life, death, and resurrection. Jesus sees the Church as created by Him.

Discussion Questions

1. Read Ephesians 5:22–33. Instead of focusing on the instructions to wives and husbands, consider what this passage teaches us about the relationship between Christ and the Church. What do we learn about how Jesus views His Bride in this text?

2. How much do you know about Church history? Do you find history interesting? Why or why not? What are some benefits to learning more about those who have gone before us in the faith?

3. In Genesis 15, God promised Abraham two things: offspring too numerous to count and a land to dwell in and possess. How do these promises find fulfillment in the Church?

4. This chapter emphasized that the Church is created by God and not by us. How can remembering this inform the way we view and participate in our own congregations?

Heavenly Father, thank You for the gift of community, for establishing us as Your people and Church. Thank You for sending Your Son as the perfect Head. Forgive us for the times when we have trusted our own strength or looked to the leadership of men instead of to the headship of our Lord Jesus. Strengthen our faith by Your Spirit so that when we look on the Church, we see not merely a collection of sinners but the Bride of Christ—a people gathered by You, beloved by You, redeemed by You, and being made holy by You. Give us Your heart not only for the lost but also for Your people, and help us to approach all people with Your compassion and love. In Jesus' name we pray. Amen.

The Rule of Faith

· ·

IRENAEUS OF LYONS

Irenaeus of Lyons was a bishop in what is now southern France. Born around AD 130, he lived only two generations after the apostles, which makes his writings especially interesting and encouraging. He was taught by a pastor named Polycarp, who had been a disciple of the apostle John. Can you imagine that? Your mentor and teacher saying to you, "The apostle John told me about the Last Supper, the night before Jesus was betrayed. He was sitting right next to the Lord Himself, and the mood in the room was . . ."

Irenaeus was a pastor and teacher of the faith and wrote a great deal about how to discern the true teachings of the Church from false teachings that were already rising up and confusing the faithful in his day. At that time, Gnostic mystery religions were culturally prominent and shaped the thinking of the people Irenaeus taught and ministered to. People commonly sought out new writings and secret letters that promised to illuminate "new mysteries" of the faith. They would have thought it strange that the greatest mysteries and truths about the one true God were available to anyone who wanted to know them. Irenaeus addressed this cultural temptation to look for new revelations by continually pointing back to the content of the faith and the apostolic roots of the Church's teachings.

In this excerpt from Irenaeus's work *Against Heresies*, he emphasizes that the Church throughout the world teaches the same message, and what she teaches is nothing other than what the apostles taught. In other words, the content of the faith defines the Church. For Irenaeus, if the content of the faith changes, that is a sign that you are no longer in the Church.

Gnosticism is the belief that the immaterial or spiritual is superior to the material. The Greek word *gnosis* means "knowledge," and Gnostic religious sects emphasized secret knowledge or revelation. They believed that our spirits are imprisoned in our bodies and that salvation means release from all physical reality.

The Church, though dispersed throughout the whole world, even to the ends of the earth, has received from the apostles and their disciples this faith: [She believes] in one God, the Father Almighty, Maker of heaven, and earth, and the sea, and all things that are in them; and in one Christ Jesus, the Son of God, who became incarnate for our salvation; and in the Holy Spirit, who proclaimed through the prophets the dispensations of God, and the advents, and the birth from a virgin, and the passion, and the resurrection from the dead, and the ascension into heaven in the flesh of the beloved Christ Jesus, our Lord, and His [future] manifestation from heaven in the glory of the Father "to gather all things in one," and to raise up anew all flesh of the whole human race, in order that to Christ Jesus, our Lord, and God, and Saviour, and

King, according to the will of the invisible Father, "every knee should bow, of things in heaven, and things in earth, and things under the earth, and that every tongue should confess" to Him, and that He should execute just judgment towards all. . . .

As I have already observed, the Church, having received this preaching and this faith, although scattered throughout the whole world, yet, as if occupying but one house, carefully preserves it. She also believes these points [of doctrine] just as if she had but one soul, and one and the same heart, and she proclaims them, and teaches them, and hands them down, with perfect harmony, as if she possessed only one mouth. For, although the languages of the world are dissimilar, yet the import of the tradition is one and the same. For the Churches which have been planted in Germany do not believe or hand down anything different, nor do those in Spain, nor those in Gaul, nor those in the East, nor those in Egypt, nor those in Libya, nor those which have been established in the central regions of the world. But as the sun, that creature of God, is one and the same throughout the whole world, so also the preaching of the truth shineth everywhere, and enlightens all men that are willing to come to a knowledge of the truth. Nor will any one of the rulers in the Churches, however highly gifted he may be in point of eloquence, teach doctrines different from these (for no one is greater than the Master); nor, on the other hand, will he who is deficient in power of expression inflict injury on the tradition. For the faith being ever one and the same, neither does one who is able at great length to discourse regarding it, make

any addition to it, nor does one, who can say but little diminish it.[7]

I love the way Irenaeus describes the Church here. "She also believes these points [of doctrine] just as if she had but one soul, and one and the same heart, and she proclaims them, and teaches them, and hands them down, with perfect harmony, as if she possessed only one mouth." What a beautiful image! Such whole-hearted, clear, without-error transmission of the faith to the next generation should be the goal for Christians in every era. The message of the Church is the same throughout the world, even though we speak different languages. Irenaeus's depiction of the Church as having one heart and soul and mouth to proclaim the Gospel reminds us of Scripture's description of the Church as one body—the Body of Christ.

Creeds vs. Deeds:
What Defines the Church?

H ave you ever heard someone described as a "good, Christian person"? Perhaps you've heard a member of an older generation use this expression, or maybe you remember it from an older movie or book. What do people mean by this description? Do they mean "an individual who clearly believes and confesses the apostolic faith as put forward in the Scriptures?" Not likely. A "good, Christian person" is usually shorthand for someone who is morally upright in the eyes of the world—someone who behaves well.

But is being a Christian about our behavior, or is it about the content of the faith? Is it about what you *do* or what you *believe*? Or

---

7   Irenaeus, *Against Heresies*, in *The Apostolic Fathers with Justin Martyr and Irenaeus*, ed. Alexander Roberts, James Donaldson, and A. Cleveland Coxe, The Ante-Nicene Fathers, vol. 1 (Buffalo, NY: Christian Literature Company, 1885), 330–31.

both? Irenaeus described the Church as a holy entity spread over the whole world whose purpose and mission is to carefully preserve the teachings of the one true faith. The content of the faith is what matters; it is how you know whether you are in the Church. Some churches and leaders today teach (either explicitly or implicitly) that the content of the faith is not as important as the behavior of the faithful. The expression "deeds not creeds" is sometimes used to summarize this philosophy. While many Christians reject such a statement (even pointing out the hypocrisy of the statement itself, as it could be considered its own short creed), we sometimes let sneakier versions of this idea into our churches.

Consider the popular statement "Preach the Gospel. If necessary, use words." The sentiment behind this expression is that the Gospel has to be lived out. Empty words not put into practice and lived out in love and care for others can push people away instead of connecting them to Jesus. In John 13:34–35, Jesus teaches His disciples:

> A new commandment I give to you, that you love one another: just as I have loved you, you also are to love one another. By this all people will know that you are My disciples, if you have love for one another.

As followers of Jesus, we are called to do what He does, and Jesus loves all people. But is doing good works what makes someone a Christian? Social organizations do many wonderful things in their communities—feed the hungry, help people find employment, care for mothers and infants, provide clothing and shelter. But would such an organization necessarily be a church? Of course not! The Gospel is not preached by actions. It may be lived out by actions, but a helping hand in a moment of need does not magically communicate the message of salvation in Christ.

Conversely, consider the account of the thief on the cross:

> One of the criminals who were hanged railed at Him,
> saying, "Are You not the Christ? Save Yourself and us!"
> But the other rebuked him, saying, "Do you not fear
> God, since you are under the same sentence of condem-
> nation? And we indeed justly, for we are receiving the
> due reward of our deeds; but this man has done nothing
> wrong." And he said, "Jesus, remember me when You
> come into Your kingdom." And He said to him, "Truly,
> I say to you, today you will be with Me in paradise."
> (Luke 23:39–43)

This man fully acknowledged that he deserved death for his deeds. But before that death came, he confessed that Jesus was Lord and placed his faith in Him for salvation. Jesus responded with beautiful words of comfort and forgiveness: "Today you will be with Me in paradise" (v. 43). This man's deeds were not "Christian." He was not a moral person. But he confessed the faith of the Church, that Jesus is Lord, and Jesus declared to him the truth that he was part of the community of the faithful. His deeds were wrong, but his creed was right!

> "If you confess with your mouth that Jesus is Lord and believe in your heart that God raised Him from the dead, you will be saved." (Romans 10:9)

The thief on the cross is a member of the Church and a perfect example of the hierarchy of creeds over deeds. We cannot be saved by what we do, but we are saved by what Jesus did on the cross. The content of the faith must be preached, or it isn't a church. We could say, "Creeds *inform* deeds," and, "Preach the Gospel. It is necessary to use words!"

Creeds as Rule of Faith

In the excerpt from Irenaeus at the start of the chapter, did you notice anything familiar? He says, "The Church . . . has received from the apostles . . . this faith," and then he summarizes the outlines of Christian doctrine. Does it sound at all like the Apostles' Creed? Irenaeus is almost as early in Church history as we can go without being in the apostolic era. In his writings, we can already see what would eventually become one of the most universally recognized statements of faith.

Just as Irenaeus did in his work *Against Heresies*, creeds have been developed historically to clarify correct doctrine and to defend against error and heresy. If you examine the words of the Apostles' Creed, you can see refutations of Gnosticism. Gnosticism believes that physical, created reality is evil and spiritual reality is good. In Gnosticism, flesh is a prison for the soul, which must be liberated from its physical bondage. Therefore, Gnostics did not believe the sovereign God would have created the world or put on human flesh and become a man or suffered; a lesser being must have done so.

The first line of the Apostles' Creed refutes the idea that God would not stoop to create a material world: "I believe in God, the Father Almighty, maker of heaven and earth." The Second Article of the Creed details how Jesus physically interacted with humanity and allowed Himself to suffer and die. An early heresy stemming from Gnostic belief suggested that Jesus was not physically present at the crucifixion but only appeared to be there. It was an attempt to reconcile these cultural misgivings. The Creed refuted those errors, confessing that yes, Jesus was truly born of a human woman, truly suffered, actually died, was really buried, and physically rose from the dead.

While we don't know the precise origin of the Apostles' Creed, we see similar language in the writings of early theologians, such as Irenaeus and Tertullian. By contrast, the history of the Nicene Creed is completely documented. It was written in AD 325 at the Council of Nicaea to safeguard the faith against the Arian heresy and adopted in its final form at the Council of Constantinople in 381.

Arianism is a false teaching that plagued the Church in the third and fourth centuries. It held that Jesus was created by the Father and was not equal to the Father or eternal in the same way the Father is eternal. The language of the Nicene Creed was carefully crafted to emphasize the equality within the Trinity, confessing that Jesus is "God of God, Light of Light, very God of very God, begotten, not made, being of one substance with the Father" (Nicene Creed).

The Church has always used creeds and confessional statements to mark the boundaries of orthodox teaching. Creeds do not summarize every point of Scripture, but they give us simple statements that allow us to say, "If you disagree with any of these points, you are professing something outside of Scripture, and you are outside of the faith of the Church." When we make this confession, our churches proclaim not only the content of our faith but also trust in the source of that content—the Bible. Confessing a creed demonstrates that we believe Scripture is clear, authoritative, and without error.

Some churches today choose not to use creeds. If you ask why, you might hear that we should not use the words of men but should rely only on the Bible, the words of God. That may seem admirable! Of course we should never add to or take away from Scripture. These churches tend to stress the ability of all Christians to read and study their Bibles on their own and come to their own understanding of Scripture. They might emphasize prayerfully reading a text and waiting to see what the Holy Spirit teaches the reader through that time. Certainly the Holy Spirit works through the Word of God to create and sustain faith in our hearts! Spending time in God's Word will strengthen our faith in and knowledge of Him.

But just because Scripture can be read by anyone does not mean we will always rightly understand it on our own or that we have the right to interpret Scripture however we want. Because of sin and our fallen, imperfect use of human reason, different people will read a text and come to different conclusions about what it says, yet there is still only one correct interpretation of any text. The Holy Spirit may use a text to apply different things to different people at different times, and texts may have layers of meaning, but there is a clarity to Scripture, and a reader's interpretation is either correct or incorrect. God intends to speak clearly to us through His Word, and it is the task of the Church to rightly understand and interpret it. The creeds help us do this. By professing a creed, we imply that the truths of Scripture are knowable, that they are not up to the individual to determine, and that they have been entrusted to the Church as a whole. Having a universal statement like a creed to safeguard the faith is comforting. It demonstrates that the message of the Church is fixed, that it cannot be changed by any one pastor or teacher for the purpose of abuse or manipulation. The rule of faith protects the assurance found in God's promises.

The Marks of the Church

C hrist has created His Church to be a beautiful, comforting community. We know this is true, but how can we tell whether any given church we attend is part of that community? Lutheran theology outlines two "marks" of the Church—two clear signs that a congregation belongs to the Body of Christ. The Augsburg Confession, written in 1530 to articulate Lutheran theology, explains these marks of the Church:

> **Our churches teach that one holy Church is to remain forever. The Church is the congregation of saints [Psalm 149:1] in which the Gospel is purely taught and the Sacraments are correctly administered. For the true unity of the Church it is enough to agree about the doctrine of the Gospel and the administration of the Sacraments. It is not necessary that human traditions, that is, rites or ceremonies instituted by men,**

should be the same everywhere. As Paul says, "One Lord, one faith, one baptism, one God and Father of all" (Ephesians 4:5–6).[8]

The first mark is that "the Gospel is purely taught." Irenaeus confessed this when he said that the Church throughout the whole world proclaims the Gospel message as with one mouth. The second mark of the Church is that "the Sacraments are correctly administered." All practices within a local congregation flow from its understanding of the Word of God. When the Word of God is rightly taught, preached, and understood, then the correct understanding of the Sacraments will naturally be present as well. The content of the faith is what makes a church *the Church.*

In 2 Timothy, Paul instructs Timothy on the central importance of teaching the Word of God in the local congregation:

Preach the word; be ready in season and out of season; reprove, rebuke, and exhort, with complete patience and teaching. For the time is coming when people will not endure sound teaching, but having itching ears they will accumulate for themselves teachers to suit their own passions, and will turn away from listening to the truth and wander off into myths. As for you, always be sober-minded, endure suffering, do the work of an evangelist, fulfill your ministry. (2 Timothy 4:2–5)

These words of Paul, written to encourage a young pastor, still reassure and instruct faithful pastors today. Pastors are called to preach the Word—to "reprove, rebuke, and exhort, with complete patience and teaching" (v. 2). When we sit down in church, we should expect to hear God's Word taught in its purity—not necessarily what we want to hear but what God wants us to hear.

---

8   Augsburg Confession VII.

Pray that God would strengthen your pastor, and all pastors, as they continue the difficult calling to teach the pure Word of God with patience.

Paul's words also provide caution and instruction for those of us who are not pastors. We live in a time when "accumulating for ourselves teachers to suit our own passions" (see v. 3) has never been easier. We can find books, sermons, and theologians who will tell us anything we want to hear. But when we consume content that teaches about the Word of God—a book, a social media post, online sermons—we should expect it to align with the rule of faith, the same truths that have been taught by orthodox Christianity throughout history.

When literally every possible message is available to us, holding fast to the pure doctrine of the Church can feel harder than ever. The Bereans in Acts 17 provide an example of how we should approach teachers of the faith with discernment:

> The brothers immediately sent Paul and Silas away by night to Berea, and when they arrived they went into the Jewish synagogue. Now these Jews were more noble than those in Thessalonica; they received the word with all eagerness, examining the Scriptures daily to see if these things were so.

Living in the internet age, we have seemingly unlimited access to all types of biblical teachers and resources. While these are surely a blessing, do not neglect the gift of your local pastor—a man who has a call from God to serve and teach you in the faith. When you read Christian books or listen to sermons or messages, be aware of the variations in different theological traditions. If you have questions about someone's teachings, use your pastor as a resource and ask him about it.

**Many of them therefore believed, with not a few Greek
women of high standing as well as men. (Acts 17:10–12)**

Like the Bereans, we should examine the Scriptures to see if what
we're being taught is biblical. And the beauty of the Church is that we
do this together, as Paul writes in his Letter to the Colossians: "Let
the word of Christ dwell in you richly, teaching and admonishing
one another in all wisdom, singing psalms and hymns and spiritual
songs, with thankfulness in your hearts to God" (3:16).

Scripture as the Highest Authority in the Church

L etting the Word of Christ dwell among us richly, as Paul says,
means giving Scripture the highest place of authority in our
churches. At the time of the Reformation, Luther and other reformers
rediscovered the doctrine of the authority of Scripture. They used
the phrase *sola Scriptura*, or "Scripture alone," as shorthand for the
belief that Scripture is the highest authority over matters of doctrine.

Sola Scriptura does not mean that Scripture is the only authority
that points us to Christ. The creeds, our confessional documents,
and the Church Fathers all have authority in the Church. Pastors
preach with authority. Parents teach their children the Word of God
with authority. But we believe Scripture is the highest authority
and the only source of authority that is without error and that can
be used to establish matters of doctrine. At the time, the reformers
were accused of innovating—creating a new article of faith—when
they suggested that Scripture alone was authoritative to establish
doctrine. But they rigorously defended this belief from God's Word
and from the writings of the Early Church Fathers. God Himself
treats the written Word this way, as we can see from Scripture.

The first account of the Word of God being committed to writing comes in Exodus 24:12, in which God tells Moses, "Come up to Me on the mountain and wait there, that I may give you the tablets of stone, with the law and the commandment, which I have written for their instruction." God is the one who first writes down His Word for His people. Throughout the Old Testament, God regularly instructs His people to write down His words and pass them on to each generation.[9] Jesus also treated the written Scriptures as sacred and authoritative in His ministry. For example, in Luke 4, Jesus read from the scroll of Isaiah and told the people that the Scriptures were being fulfilled as He spoke. In Mark 7, He chastised the Pharisees for elevating the traditions of men over the Scriptures. Jesus' earthly ministry bears witness to God's desire for us to have the Word in writing. In the last chapters of the Bible, Jesus again states God's intent regarding His Word: "He who was seated on the throne said, 'Behold, I am making all things new.' Also He said, 'Write this down, for these words are trustworthy and true'" (Revelation 21:5).

Some denominations do not give Scripture the highest position of authority. Roman Catholic Christians, for example, hold to a two-source view of authority, granting equal authority to Church tradition as they do to written Scripture. They defend this position by arguing that determining which books are in the Bible is already an appeal to Church tradition. After all, was not the canon of Scripture determined by the Church Fathers? If the Church decides what is canonical and what is not, wouldn't this mean that the Church is ultimately the highest authority?

> The word *canon* comes from a Greek word meaning "rule" or "measuring stick." It refers to the list of books considered to be the authoritative Word of God.

---

9   See, for example, Exodus 34:27; Deuteronomy 27:8; Isaiah 30:8; Jeremiah 30:2; Ezekiel 43:11; and Habakkuk 2:2.

Lutherans challenge this argument. The writings of the Early Church Fathers make it clear that no one person took upon themselves the authority to determine which books were in the Bible and which were not. Instead, as writings began to circulate that were clearly not correct in their teaching—for example, the Gnostic gospels and other books that did not confess Jesus as Lord—the faithful within the Church compiled lists of which books were agreed upon by all to be correct and from the apostles. These early lists simply put in writing which books were being used as Scripture in trusted churches that taught the apostolic faith. No single person, council, or committee sat down and established the canon of Scripture. Rather, the books that were clearly scriptural were recognized by the faithful as such. To be canonical, a book of the Bible must have been written by either an apostle or a prophet (someone who received the revelation directly from God), it must proclaim Jesus Christ, and it must have been recognized as authoritative by the Early Church (meaning it was used in the worship services of early congregations).

> When churches call themselves "apostolic," not all churches mean the same thing by it. When Lutherans say that our church is apostolic, we mean that it teaches the same doctrine that was taught and put into writing by the apostles. This apostolic faith is found in the Holy Scriptures.

Martin Chemnitz, a second-generation Lutheran theologian, wrote an exhaustive refutation of the Roman Catholic position in his four-volume work *An Examination of the Council of Trent*. He cited numerous Church Fathers who upheld the authority of Scripture over oral traditions or additional revelations of doctrine. In the following quotation, Chemnitz cites Irenaeus, who ties the authority of Scripture to the apostles' intent. Irenaeus argues that the apostles wrote the books of the New Testament knowing they would become the final rule of faith for future generations. When people die, they can still speak to us authoritatively through their writings. Thus, the eyewitness accounts of Jesus Christ and His life, death, and resurrection live on in the writings of the New Testament.

> Irenaeus says: "The apostles delivered to us in the Scriptures what they had preached." And for what purpose? What use did the apostles want the church to make of this their Scripture? Irenaeus answers: "That that which they delivered to us in writing might in the future be the foundation and pillar of our faith," namely, of that faith which the church received from the apostles and delivered to her children. Therefore we have in the Scriptures which the apostles delivered to us by the will of God the foundation and pillar of the only true and life-giving faith of the primitive church, received from the apostles. It is called the foundation of faith, because faith is learned, known, built up, and received from it. It is called a pillar because through it that faith which alone is true and gives life is proved, confirmed, defended against all corruptions, and preserved. A faith, therefore, which is built up, received, proved, and confirmed from any other source than from the Scriptures transmitted by the apostles is not the true, life-giving, apostolic faith of the primitive church.[10]

Summarized, the faith of the apostles is the faith of the Scriptures. The Bible is where we find the Church's teachings in their purity. Later in the same work, Chemnitz beautifully articulates the connection between the Scripture and the true Church:

---

10   Martin Chemnitz, *Examination of the Council of Trent*, Part 1, trans. Fred Kramer, *Chemnitz's Works*, vol. 1 (St. Louis: Concordia Publishing House, 2007), 81–82.

> It is as true as it can be that the true church cannot be separated from the true doctrine of faith. For that is the true church which embraces and confesses the true and sound doctrine of the Word of God. But when that body of men which has the title of the church departs from the true doctrine of the Word of God, it does not follow on that account, either that the sound doctrine is false, or that the errors, which that body of men holds, are the truth; but this follows, that that body of men, when it no longer has the true doctrine, is not the true church. *Therefore the truth of the Word of God does not depend on the church, . . . but on the contrary, the truth of the church depends on and is judged by the truth of the Word of God, which it holds and confesses.*[11]

That last sentence is what we mean by *sola Scriptura*. We need the comfort and certainty that comes from Jesus Christ, and He speaks to us through His Word in Scripture. The Church is the true Church when the Word of God is taught in its purity. Comfort and assurance are always grounded in truth. Jesus is the truth (John 14:6); therefore, true comfort comes from God's Word. The Church, then, serves to amplify the Word of God over and above all other words and ideas among God's people. This is the only way to rightly know who we are and who our God is.

What does this look like in practice? It means we should seek out congregations that teach Scripture. Many church bodies are not faithful to God's Word, but we should expect our churches to hold Scripture sacred and teach it, even when doing so is hard or unpopular. Confessional statements help us do this. Most churches say they believe and teach the Bible, but what do they believe the Bible says? Their confession of faith will tell you. The confessional

---

11 Chemnitz, *Examination of the Council of Trent*, vol. 1, 163, emphasis added.

statements of the Lutheran Church, for example, are contained in the Book of Concord. These statements are not equivalent to Scripture—they are written by mere men—but they explain in a straightforward way what our churches teach concerning the Word of God. Confessional statements let us know what a church will be teaching, preaching, and living out in their communities.

I encourage you to explore what your congregation confesses about Scripture. Not all churches are the same, even ones that claim to love Jesus and believe the Bible. What churches believe *about* Jesus and the Bible varies widely! As Christians, we should take the Word of God seriously, studying it carefully like the Bereans, using it to safeguard ourselves and our churches against error, and finding comfort in the Gospel message we read there. Jesus came for us! He wants us to know Him. And He speaks to us through His Word.

Final Thought

The concept of the rule of faith can sound restrictive, like stuffy doctrinal rigidness or ideological arrogance. But this is not why we have the rule of faith. We proclaim and defend the true teachings of Scripture because in those words we hear the heart of God for His people. As members of the Church that confesses the faith of the apostles and the faith put forth in Scripture, we have

Perhaps this chapter leaves you wondering about denominational divides. Thankfully, we do not have to understand God's Word perfectly to be saved. Our certainty rests in Christ, not in our own understanding. We will explore this tension more thoroughly in chapter 6.

comfort and security, knowing the Word of God dwells among us richly. Jesus describes the life-giving, comforting peace that comes from a life immersed in His Word in John 8:31–32: "If you abide in

My word, you are truly My disciples, and you will know the truth, and the truth will set you free." Jesus sees the Church as the children of God abiding in His Word.

Discussion Questions

. . . .

1. What do these Scripture passages say about how our churches should approach the Word of God?

   - 2 Corinthians 6:14
   - John 8:31–32
   - John 15:5

2. What are some warning signs that might indicate a false teacher?

3. Read 2 Peter 1:18–21. What does it mean in this passage that "no prophecy of Scripture comes from someone's own interpretation" (v. 20)?

4. Read John 8:31–47. What does Jesus say about those who abide in His Word? What does He say about those who "cannot bear to hear [His] word" (v. 43)? What is Jesus teaching us here about what it means to be children of God?

Dear Lord Jesus, in the Book of John, we read that You are the Word of God, that You have been at work in our world since the very beginning, and that You became flesh to dwell among us. We also read that being Your disciples means abiding in Your Word. Lord, forgive us for those times when we have not prioritized abiding in Your Word. Forgive us for times when we have elevated other words and ideas in our lives and put off spending time with You in Your Word. Send the Holy Spirit to speak to us through Your Word, to nurture our faith, and to transform us each day to be more like You. In Your holy name we pray. Amen.

The Fellowship
of the Saints

······································

Born in AD 315, Cyril served as Bishop of Jerusalem from around 350 until his death in 386. He lived during the height of the Arian controversy (mentioned in chapter 2). The Church condemned Arianism at the Council of Nicaea in 325 and again at the Council of Constantinople in 381. During the intermittent era, Arian and orthodox emperors and bishops vied for control of the Church. Cyril was a faithful pastor and teacher, but because he lived during a time of such political and doctrinal controversy, he was exiled from Jerusalem and then restored three times as the politics in his region vacillated. He is best known for the orthodoxy of his teaching and for his series of catechetical lectures.

Cyril's catechetical, or teaching, lectures were used to instruct adult converts before their Baptism and confirmation into the Church. They are strikingly similar to our current adult confirmation or new member classes. In the lectures, which were likely recorded by scribes as Cyril spoke, he teaches his way through the Nicene Creed, instructing on each point of doctrine: confession and forgiveness, Baptism, and the Lord's Supper. The lectures took place during Lent, leading up to the Baptism and confirmation of the converts at the Easter Vigil service, which was the custom of the Church at the time and is still customary in many churches today.

The word *catholic* most properly means "universal" or "whole." Many churches today use the word *Christian* instead of *catholic* in the Creed. Regardless of the version used, we profess belief in the universal Church spread throughout the world.

In this excerpt from his Lecture 18, Cyril teaches on the phrase "And one holy Catholic Church" from the Nicene Creed. The Creed goes straight from "I believe in the Holy Spirit, the Holy Catholic Church" to "the communion of saints." Cyril shows how these two concepts are united: the Holy Spirit transforms us from many individuals into the singular Body of Christ.

It is called Catholic then because it extends over all the world, from one end of the earth to the other; and because it teaches universally and completely one and all the doctrines which ought to come to men's knowledge, concerning things both visible and invisible, heavenly and earthly; and because it brings into subjection to godliness the whole race of mankind, governors and governed, learned and unlearned; and because it universally treats and heals the whole class of sins, which are committed by soul or body, and possesses in itself every form of virtue which is named, both in deeds and words, and in every kind of spiritual gifts.

And it is rightly named (Ecclesia) because it calls forth and assembles together all men; according as the Lord says in Leviticus, *And make an assembly for all the congregation at the door of the tabernacle of witness.* And it is to be noted, that the word *assemble*, is used for the first time in the Scriptures here, at the time when the Lord puts Aaron into the High-priesthood. . . .

But since the word Ecclesia is applied to different things (as also it is written of the multitude in the theatre of the Ephesians, *And when he had thus spoken, he dismissed the Assembly*), and since one might properly and truly say that there is a Church of evil doers, I mean the meetings of the heretics, the Marcionists and Manichees, and the rest, for this cause the Faith has securely delivered to thee now the Article, "And in one Holy Catholic Church;" that thou mayest avoid their wretched meetings, and ever abide with the Holy Church Catholic in which thou wast regenerated. And if ever thou art sojourning in cities, inquire not simply where the Lord's House is (for the other sects of the profane also attempt to call their own dens houses of the Lord), nor merely where the Church is, but where is the Catholic Church.

> The Marcionites and Manichees were both Gnostic heretical sects in the early centuries of the Church. The Marcionites taught that the god of the Old Testament who created the world was an angry god and separate from Jesus, the god of the New Testament. They rejected the entire Old Testament and much of the New Testament. The Manichees taught a complex cosmic system of light versus dark, where the spiritual is good and all physical things are evil.

For this is the peculiar name of this Holy Church, the mother of us all, which is the spouse of our Lord Jesus Christ, The Only-begotten Son of God (for it is written, *As Christ also loved the Church and gave Himself for it*, and all the rest,) and is a figure and copy of *Jerusalem which is above, which is free, and the mother of us all*; which before was barren, but now has many children. . . .

And while the kings of particular nations have bounds set to their authority, the Holy Church Catholic alone extends her power without limit over the whole world; *for God*, as it is written, *hath made her border peace*. But I should need many more hours for my discourse, if I wished to speak of all things which concern her.

In this Holy Catholic Church receiving instruction and behaving ourselves virtuously, we shall attain the kingdom of heaven, and inherit ETERNAL LIFE; for which also we endure all toils, that we may be made partakers thereof from the Lord. For ours is no trifling aim, but our endeavour is for eternal life. Wherefore in the profession of the Faith, after the words, "AND IN THE RESURRECTION OF THE FLESH," that is, of the dead (of which we have discoursed), we are taught to believe also "IN THE LIFE ETERNAL," for which as Christians we are striving.[12]

Cyril makes it obvious that we are not alone, left to struggle in our Christian walk by ourselves, independent of one another. We are a fellowship drawn together by the Holy Spirit and united

---

12   Cyril of Jerusalem, Lecture 18, in *S. Cyril of Jerusalem, S. Gregory Nazianzen*, ed. Philip Schaff and Henry Wace, A Select Library of the Nicene and Post-Nicene Fathers of the Christian Church, second series, vol. 7 (New York: The Christian Literature Company, 1894), 139–41.

with Christ as His Body, with the rule of faith as our rallying cry. For our purposes, two specific points from the excerpt stand out.

First, Cyril emphasizes the familial nature of the Church. He describes the Church both as "the mother of us all" and as "the spouse of our Lord Jesus Christ." This familial reality centers on the way Jesus unites us to Himself. As the Church, we are collectively the Bride of Christ, redeemed and made blameless by Him. But the Church also holds each individual Christian as a mother would, nurturing and raising us in the family of God. Scripture uses both types of language—maternal and bridal—to describe the Church, and faithful Christians, including Cyril and other Church Fathers, profess this as well.

Second, Cyril makes the connection between doctrine and practice. He says, "In this Holy Catholic Church *receiving instruction and behaving ourselves virtuously,* we shall attain the kingdom of heaven, and inherit eternal life" (emphasis added). These two aspects of the Christian life go together. As Irenaeus did before him, Cyril emphasizes the central role of the rule of faith, adding to this the conviction that our actions should flow from our beliefs.

Cyril expounds on this in an earlier lecture: "For the method of godliness consists of these two things, pious doctrines, and virtuous practice: and neither are the doctrines acceptable to God apart from good works, nor does God accept the works which are not perfected with pious doctrines."[13] He goes on to explain that it is of no value to live a virtuous life and yet not believe in God; neither is it possible to retain your faith while living an unrepentant life of sin. That is why, according to Cyril, Christians should be taught the creeds. Through them, we

---

13   Cyril of Jerusalem, Lecture 4, in *S. Cyril of Jerusalem, S. Gregory Nazianzen,* 19.

learn the teachings of the Church and will be protected against heresy. We also learn how we are to live as the Body of Christ.[14]

Pentecost and the Birth of the Church

· · · · · · · · · · · · · · · · · ·

So far, we have seen that Jesus is the Head of the Church and that the truth about Jesus and what He has done for us is held supreme above all else in His Church. We know that Jesus' Word is powerful and performative—it accomplishes what it says it does. But how does this Word forge the Church as the fellowship of the saints? The Book of Acts describes what happened to Jesus' followers after He ascended into heaven. They grew from a small group of disciples to a worldwide community of the faithful. In Acts 1, we read Jesus' final words to His disciples before He ascended to the right hand of God:

> And while staying with them He ordered them not to depart from Jerusalem, but to wait for the promise of the Father, which, He said, "you heard from Me; for John baptized with water, but you will be baptized with the Holy Spirit not many days from now." So when they had come together, they asked Him, "Lord, will You at this time restore the kingdom to Israel?" He said to them, "It is not for you to know times or seasons that the Father has fixed by His own authority. But you will receive power when the Holy Spirit has come upon you, and you will be My witnesses in Jerusalem and in all Judea and Samaria, and to the end of the earth."

---

14   Cyril lived at the time when the Nicene Creed was first formulated and accepted by the Church, so his teachings on the use and purpose of the Creed in the congregation are of historical interest.

> **And when He had said these things, as they were look-
> ing on, He was lifted up, and a cloud took Him out of
> their sight. (Acts 1:4–9)**

All three persons of the Trinity are present in verses 4–5. Jesus
is the one instructing His disciples, but He points to the Father's
authority over all things. The Holy Spirit is sent as promised by the
Father, and the Father alone ordains the times and seasons of history. All three persons of the Trinity were present at creation, yet
we associate creation with the role of the Father. All three persons
are present in redemption, yet we associate redemption with the
work of the Son. Similarly, though all three persons are present in
the birth of the Christian Church, we associate the Church most
closely with the Holy Spirit. Jesus told His disciples that once the
Holy Spirit came, they would be His witnesses to the ends of the
earth. The Holy Spirit's work in the Church *is* the Church. There is
simply no Church without Him.

In Acts 2, the Spirit was poured out on the disciples just as Jesus
promised. This outpouring led to the first church sermon. Peter
declared to the Jews gathered for Pentecost that Jesus is the fulfillment of the Old Testament, the promised Messiah. He invoked the
prophet Joel, who preached, "And in the last days it shall be, God
declares, that I will pour out My Spirit on all flesh. . . . And it shall
come to pass that everyone who calls upon the name of the Lord
shall be saved" (Acts 2:17, 21). This is the Good News that salvation
is for all people in Christ, not only for the Jews. Peter traces Old
Testament prophecy to demonstrate that Jesus is the Promised One
of David's line who was foretold. He concludes, "Let all the house
of Israel therefore know for certain that God has made Him both
Lord and Christ, this Jesus whom you crucified" (2:36).

Through Peter's declaration of the Word, the Holy Spirit worked
in the hearts of those who heard:

> When [the people] heard this they were cut to the heart,
> and said to Peter and the rest of the apostles, "Brothers,
> what shall we do?" And Peter said to them, "Repent and
> be baptized every one of you in the name of Jesus Christ
> for the forgiveness of your sins, and you will receive the
> gift of the Holy Spirit. For the promise is for you and
> for your children and for all who are far off, everyone
> whom the Lord our God calls to Himself." (2:37–39)

They were cut to the heart. This is the work of the Holy Spirit. He convicts us of sin and draws us to knowledge of Christ. Heartbroken to learn that the man they had crucified was in fact their Savior, three thousand souls received the Gospel and were baptized that day. We then read a description of the life of this earliest Church: "They devoted themselves to the apostles' teaching and the fellowship, to the breaking of bread and the prayers" (2:42).

> The "breaking of bread" mentioned in Acts 2:42 is likely a reference to Communion. See Acts 20:7: "On the first day of the week, when we were gathered together to break bread . . ."

From the very beginning, the Church was grounded in fellowship—devoted to the apostles' teaching through the worship life of the congregation.

The New Life in Christ

The entire six-chapter Book of Ephesians paints a picture of what life in the Body of Christ will look like. In chapter 4, Paul speaks of the unity we share: "There is one body and one Spirit—just as you were called to the one hope that belongs to your call—one Lord, one faith, one baptism" (vv. 4–5). There is only one God, and we are made one in Him when we are gathered into the arms of the Church through Baptism. Paul goes on to discuss the various spiritual gifts that are given to members of the Church, not for the purpose of glorifying individuals, but rather "for building up the body of Christ" (4:12). God gives us these gifts so we may become spiritually mature. This maturity comes when we rightly understand the doctrine of our faith and live that faith out in love. Ephesians 4, quoted at length, demonstrates the connection between the Body of Christ and our growth into more mature Christians.

> So that we may no longer be children, tossed to and fro by the waves and carried about by every wind of doctrine, by human cunning, by craftiness in deceitful schemes. Rather, speaking the truth in love, we are to grow up in every way into Him who is the head, into Christ, from whom the whole body, joined and held together by every joint with which it is equipped, when each part is working properly, makes the body grow so that it builds itself up in love. Now this I say and testify in the Lord, that you must no longer walk as the Gentiles do, in the futility of their minds. They are darkened in their understanding, alienated from the life of God because of the ignorance that is in them, due to their hardness of heart. They have become callous and have given themselves up to sensuality, greedy to practice every kind of impurity. But that is not the way you learned Christ!—assuming that you have heard about Him and were taught in Him, as the truth is in Jesus, to put off your old self, which belongs to your former manner of life and is corrupt through deceitful desires, and to be renewed in the spirit of your minds, and to put on the new self, created after the likeness of God in true righteousness and holiness. (vv. 14–24)

This passage sets the bar for the life of the Christian. Now that we are in Christ, we are not to "walk as the Gentiles do" (v. 17). The knowledge of the truth—that Jesus has redeemed us and forgiven our sins—necessitates living out our faith. Faith is not merely an intellectual assent to a list of truth claims. The kind of faith that saves is trust in the promises of Jesus. When we trust Jesus as our Lord, our lives will be marked by obedience to Him and a delight in God's will for us and His design for our lives. The Augsburg Confession expresses this well: "Our churches teach that this faith is bound to bring forth good fruit [Galatians 5:22–23]. It is necessary to do good works commanded by God [Ephesians 2:10], because of God's will."[15] When Jesus is your Lord, obedience to Him is truly necessary.

> Jesus doesn't demand our obedience as a condition of our salvation. Rather, He redeems us first, and then He sends His Spirit to help us to follow Him. "But God shows His love for us in that while we were still sinners, Christ died for us" (Romans 5:8).

Consider the analogy of children and parents. When you are a child and live at home with your parents, certain works are necessary. Your parents do not exaggerate or speak incorrectly if they tell you that you *have* to clean your room or you *have* to be kind to your brother or sister. Because you are their child, these things are required. But doing these things does not make you a member of the family. You are not their child *because* you clean your room or *because* you are kind to your brother or sister. Your actions within the home do not determine your status. Likewise, if a strange kid wanders into the house and starts cleaning and is pleasant to everyone, that does not make him a member of the family.

God's family is like that too. You can't earn your way in. But for those of us who are in, out of love, honor, and respect for our Lord,

---

15 Augsburg Confession VI 1.

we have a desire (born of the Spirit's work in us) to do what He says. We do not always succeed in obeying our Lord, just as even the best of children do not always obey their parents or behave kindly toward their siblings. As Paul describes, there are two desires at war within us: the desire to sin and the desire not to sin (Romans 7:22–23). Yet just as families help us grow in virtue and obedience, so also, the family of God—the Church—is a good gift that God uses to help us grow in Him.

Sanctification:
The Holy Spirit at Work

In the Large Catechism, Luther starts his explanation of the Third Article of the Apostle's Creed this way: "I cannot connect this article . . . to anything better than Sanctification. Through this article the Holy Spirit, with His office, is declared and shown: He makes people holy."[16] Sanctification is the process of becoming more holy. It is the process through which Christians learn to live according to God's design and grow in their trust in God and ability to keep God's laws. Sanctification is not the same as justification. While sanctification is a process, justification is not. Justification is God's *declaration* that we are free of guilt—the courtroom-like verdict of innocence that is ours because of Jesus' atoning work on the cross. We are saved by grace "through faith. And this is not your own doing; it is the gift of God, not a result of works, so that no one may boast" (Ephesians 2:8–9).

> "I believe in the Holy Spirit, the holy Christian Church, the communion of saints, the forgiveness of sins, the resurrection of the body, and the life everlasting. Amen." (Apostles' Creed, Third Article)

---

16   Large Catechism II 35.

Although good works do not save us, they will nonetheless be present in the life of a believer.

The Augsburg Confession articulates it this way: "Our churches teach that this faith is bound to bring forth good fruit [Galatians 5:22–23]. It is necessary to do good works commanded by God [Ephesians 2:10], because of God's will. We should not rely on those works to merit justification before God. The forgiveness of sins and justification is received through faith."[17]

The process of sanctification is also not our own work. The Holy Spirit enacts this transformation in us, and sanctification takes place in the context of the Church. The Third Article of the Creed expresses this as belief in "the communion of saints." The word *saint* refers to those who have been made righteous before God. Luther explains:

> The Holy Spirit causes our sanctification by the follow-
> ing: the communion of saints or the Christian Church,
> the forgiveness of sins, the resurrection of the body,
> and the life everlasting. That means He leads us first
> into His holy congregation and places us in the bosom
> of the Church. Through the Church He preaches to us
> and brings us to Christ.[18]

When God's Word is preached in the Church, the Holy Spirit works in our hearts through that Word. Jesus' Word is performative—it does what it says it will do! Jesus is the Word made flesh, and we encounter Him at church in both the preached Word and in His Supper, where He gives us His body and blood. Luther goes on to explain that the Holy Spirit makes each of us holy

> by the Christian Church, the forgiveness of sins, the
> resurrection of the body, and the life everlasting. For
> in the first place, the Spirit has His own congregation

17 Augsburg Confession VI 1–2.
18 Large Catechism II 37.

in the world, which is the mother that conceives and bears every Christian through God's Word [Galatians 4:26]. Through the Word He reveals and preaches, He illuminates and enkindles hearts, so that they understand, accept, cling to, and persevere in the Word [1 Corinthians 2:12].[19]

Luther includes "the resurrection of the body, and the life everlasting" in his description of sanctification. Indeed, if sanctification is the process of becoming holy and more like Christ, it culminates and ultimately concludes in the resurrection and life to come. We may become more Christlike in this life, but the process cannot be completed this side of eternity. This is a paradox—the tension of the now and the not yet. The Church must balance this tension, holding us to God's standard while offering us forgiveness when we fall short. Many churches struggle with this, either emphasizing God's grace to the point of holding members to no standards or emphasizing the standard so strongly that people despair of God's grace. We can turn to the instructions given to the New Testament Church for guidance in understanding this balance.

In 2 Thessalonians 1:3, Paul says, "We ought always to give thanks to God for you, brothers, as is right, because your faith is growing abundantly, and the love of every one of you for one another is increasing." Acts 5 recounts the tragic story of Ananias and Sapphira; they lied to God and to His Church about donating the proceeds of their property sale to the church, and they both dropped dead. When this happened, "great fear came upon the whole church and upon all who heard of these

> "But the Helper, the Holy Spirit, whom the Father will send in My name, He will teach you all things and bring to your remembrance all that I have said to you." (John 14:26)

---

19   Large Catechism II 41–42.

things" (v. 11). In Matthew 18, Jesus instructed His disciples about their great responsibility as leaders in the Church: "Whoever receives one such child in My name receives Me, but whoever causes one of these little ones who believe in Me to sin, it would be better for him to have a great millstone fastened around his neck and to be drowned in the depth of the sea" (vv. 5–6). John writes, "If we say we have fellowship with Him while we walk in darkness, we lie and do not practice the truth. But if we walk in the light, as He is in the light, we have fellowship with one another, and the blood of Jesus His Son cleanses us from all sin" (1 John 1:6–7). The bar is high for God's people! But thankfully, we do not live up to this standard on our own strength. Jesus describes the Holy Spirit as our Helper. What good news!

The goal of our life in the Church is to become spiritually mature. As Paul says in Colossians, "Him we proclaim, warning everyone and teaching everyone with all wisdom, that we may present everyone mature in Christ" (1:28). Believers are held to a high standard for two reasons: First, God's design for us is good, and the Holy Spirit enables us to live in obedience to Him for our own benefit. Second, Jesus wants all people who encounter His Body, the Church, to encounter Him. The Church is an embassy of the new creation. When Jesus taught in His parables that "the kingdom of heaven is at hand" (Matthew 4:17), He meant that in His Church and His followers,

> "So then you are no longer strangers and aliens, but you are fellow citizens with the saints and members of the household of God, built on the foundation of the apostles and prophets, Christ Jesus Himself being the cornerstone, in whom the whole structure, being joined together, grows into a holy temple in the Lord. In Him you also are being built together into a dwelling place for God by the Spirit." (Ephesians 2:19–22)

the kingdom has already begun—another part of the now and not yet.

Because the Church is meant to point all those who encounter her to Christ, it is not a place for individualistic thinking or pride. When we gather as the Church, we must be humble, as our servant-Lord modeled for us. We must focus not on our own preferences or desires but on the truth of God's Word, the needs of others, and the work of the Holy Spirit among us. This means that, practically speaking, we must be willing to be corrected by God's Word if we discover we have been in error or ignorant of His design for us. It also means we must give up our personal preferences if they are not best for the health of the Body of Christ as a whole.

We hold one another to these standards out of love. We especially hold our pastors and leaders to them because they represent the entire Church in their conduct and teaching. When pastors or church leaders fail to live up to the scriptural standards for their office, it is right for them to step down. This does not mean they are unforgivable, unlovable, or a less-valued member of the Body. However, by humbly submitting to Scripture's guidance on qualifications for ministry, they can model to the whole congregation submission to God's Word and the fruit of repentance. (We will cover the responsibilities and roles of the pastoral office in more depth in chapter 5.)

Perhaps you have been hurt by the Church or the sins of people who claim to represent Christ. If this is you, know that you are right to be upset. When a person representing our good and loving God betrays our trust, it shakes our faith. If those who have hurt us are supposed to image God's authority or presence in our lives, it is no surprise when their transgressions cause us to doubt God. The Church is meant to be heaven on earth, yet we live in the tension that the Church is full of sinners. When our faith is shaken because of the Church's betrayal, we must look back to Christ, the one who sanctifies us. He is the one who washes us clean and loves us perfectly as no fellow sinner can.

Why You Need the Church

I f we only preach that "Jesus loves you and died for you," we are missing the *why* of the story. It is true—Jesus loves *you* as an individual and died for *you* so that you could live forever with Him. But He did not die only to save you from eternal separation from God; He came to restore all of creation to perfection. On the Last Day, when Christ returns in glory, all will be as it should be, and we will be perfect, able to perfectly follow God's Law and live according to His good design. More than merely an escape from a broken world, God's plan is redemptive. It is in God's nature to fix what has been broken and to redeem what has been lost. Before humanity's fall into sin, we were designed to abide in God's Word and to live according to His Law. As the embassy of the new creation to come, the Church is the fellowship of believers in which God is already restoring us as His people.

> "Then I saw a new heaven and a new earth, for the first heaven and the first earth had passed away, and the sea was no more. And I saw the holy city, new Jerusalem, coming down out of heaven from God, prepared as a bride adorned for her husband. And I heard a loud voice from the throne saying, 'Behold, the dwelling place of God is with man. He will dwell with them, and they will be His people.' . . . And He who was seated on the throne said, 'Behold, I am making all things new.'" (Revelation 21:1–3, 5)

At the beginning of this chapter, we read Cyril's words, describing the Church as "the mother of us all." A good mother provides for our needs, loves us unconditionally, brings us up in the knowledge of God, and feeds us the foods we need to grow. The Church does this for us too. Luther speaks of the Church as the place where sanctification occurs, where we receive forgiveness and are made holy:

> However, while sanctification has begun and is growing daily [2 Thessalonians 1:3], we expect that our flesh will be destroyed and buried with all its uncleanness [Romans 6:4–11]. Then we will come forth gloriously and arise in a new, eternal life of entire and perfect holiness. For now we are only half pure and holy. So the Holy Spirit always has some reason to continue His work in us through the Word. He must daily administer forgiveness until we reach the life to come. At that time there will be no more forgiveness, but only perfectly pure and holy people [1 Corinthians 13:10]. We will be full of godliness and righteousness, removed and free from sin, death, and all evil, in a new, immortal, and glorified body [1 Corinthians 15:43, 53].[20]

The blessings we experience in the Church are a foretaste of our lives to come in the new creation. In that future, we will not be alone. We are not left alone today either. God has given us the fellowship of the saints to strengthen our faith. Within that fellowship, He has given His gifts of the Word and the Sacraments to be tangibly present with us from now until Christ returns in glory.

Final Thought

The Church is the community of the faithful. When we gather together around the Word of God properly proclaimed and the Sacraments as instituted by Jesus, our Lord uses these gifts to strengthen our faith and build us into His Body. When we gather, we represent Christ to one another as He has instructed us; that is

---

20   Large Catechism II 57–58.

how God means for people to encounter Him. The practices of the Church as a community are therefore very important, which is why we do not shy away from preaching God's Law and why Scripture exhorts us to teach carefully and practice our faith rightly. The practices of the Church matter because we are called to be the Body of Christ. And yet, it is not us working to become more holy but the Holy Spirit who produces His fruit in our hearts and lives. In the Church, we are not alone but are made into one Body by our Savior. Jesus sees the Church as the fellowship of believers strengthened and sanctified by the Holy Spirit.

Discussion Questions

· ·

1. Read Acts 2:42–47. This text describes the earliest Church. How can you see the Holy Spirit at work in this passage? What else do you notice about the Early Church in this text?

2. What are some ways that the Church builds you up in your faith? What are some things you would miss if you could no longer gather together with the Body of Christ?

3. In chapter 2, we talked about God's Word and the centrality of the rule of faith in the Church. What is the connection between God's Word and the Holy Spirit's sanctifying work in the Church?

4. Read Romans 6:1–14. What does this passage teach us about living as God's people in light of our Baptism? How are we to respond to our own sin now that we have been made part of God's family?

Holy Spirit, the apostles were told by Jesus to go to Jerusalem and wait for the Helper to come. They were instructed to do nothing without You. Thank You for the promise of Your presence in our lives, sealed by our Baptism. We repent of those times when we have not valued Your work in our hearts. We ask forgiveness for our unrepentance, our pride, and our belief (whether conscious or unconscious) that we can do good works on our own apart from You. Work through Your promised means, Spirit, through the Word and the Sacraments, to sanctify us, to make us more like our Savior, Jesus Christ, in whose name we pray. Amen.

The Universal
Church

AUGUSTINE OF HIPPO

One of the most well-known Church Fathers, Augustine is responsible for shaping much of the theological tradition of the Western Church. He was born in Thagaste, North Africa, in AD 354 and raised by his mother, Monica, a pious Christian woman who prayed earnestly for his conversion to Christianity. For many years, he was caught up in Manichaeism, a prophetic, Gnostic religious group that taught a dramatic, eternal struggle between the good, spiritual forces and the evil, material forces in our world. Augustine famously recounted his struggles with faith and with the nature of God in his autobiographical work *Confessions*, in which he shares his conversion story and marvels at the nature of the Christian God and the teachings of Scripture. He was converted and baptized into the Christian Church in 386, ultimately serving as Bishop of Hippo, a city in North Africa across the Mediterranean Sea from Italy, until his death in 430.

Augustine was a bishop during the fall of Rome. Perhaps because he witnessed an era of comfort and stability for the Church start to crumble as Roman civilization began to fail, Augustine emphasized the universal, lasting, enduring nature of the Church in his writings and teachings. His other most well-known work, *The City of God*, explores the distinction between the heavenly kingdom of God and the earthly city of man. While man-made kingdoms do not last, the heavenly kingdom that is the Church will never perish.

In one sermon, Augustine presents that timeless truth this way:

This the disciples did not yet see: they did not yet see the Church throughout all nations, beginning at Jerusalem. They saw the Head, and they believed the Head touching the Body. By this which they saw, they believed that which they saw not. We too are like to them: we see something which they saw not, and something we do not see which they did see. *What do we see, which they saw not? The Church throughout all nations. What do we not see, which they saw? Christ present in the flesh. As they saw Him, and believed concerning the Body, so do we see the Body; let us believe concerning the Head. Let what we have respectively seen help us. The sight of Christ helped them to believe the future Church: the sight of the Church helps us to believe that Christ has risen.* Their faith was made complete, and ours is made complete also. Their faith was made complete from the sight of the Head, ours is made complete by the sight of the Body. Christ was made known to them "wholly," and to us is He so made known: but He was not seen "wholly" by them, nor by us has He been "wholly" seen. By them the Head was seen, the Body believed. By us the

Body has been seen, the Head believed. Yet to none is Christ lacking: in all He is complete, though to this day His Body remains imperfect. The Apostles believed; through them many of the inhabitants of Jerusalem believed; Judea believed. Samaria believed. Let the members be added on, the building added on to the foundation. . . .

Spread the Gospel: scatter with thy mouth what thou hast conceived in thine heart. Let the nations hear, let the nations believe; let the nations multiply, let the Lord's empurpled spouse spring forth from the blood of Martyrs. And from her how many have come already, how many members have cleaved to the Head, and cleave to Him still and believe! They were baptized, and others shall be baptized, and after them shall others come. Then I say, at the end of the world shall the stones be joined to the foundation, living stones, holy stones, that at the end the whole edifice may be built by that Church, yea by this very Church which now sings the new song, while the house is in building. For so the Psalm itself says, "When the house was in building after the captivity;" and what says it, "Sing unto the Lord a new song, sing unto the Lord all the earth." How great a house is this! But when does it sing the new song? When it is in building. When is it dedicated? At the end of the world. Its foundation has been already dedicated, because He hath ascended into heaven, and dieth no more. When we too shall have risen to die no more, then shall we be dedicated.[21]

---

21 Augustine of Hippo, "Sermons on Selected Lessons of the New Testament," in *Saint Augustine: Sermon on the Mount, Harmony of the Gospels, Homilies on the Gospels,* ed. Philip Schaff, A Select Library of the Nicene and Post-Nicene Fathers of the Christian Church, first series, vol. 6 (New York: Christian Literature Company, 1888), 457–58, emphasis added.

Here Augustine links the existence of the visible, universal Church with the hope that we have in Christ. When he says, "By them the Head was seen, the Body believed. By us the Body has been seen, the Head believed," he reminds us that the apostles, like us, had to have faith in something that they could not see. Before His ascension, Jesus promised His disciples that His Body would extend throughout the entire world and would exist forever until all things are united with Him in His return. At that time, the disciples were few in number and had not yet received the Holy Spirit on Pentecost. The apostles could not see this Church extending throughout the world, but they saw Jesus, the Head, and believed in the Body by faith. We cannot see Jesus in the flesh, but we can see the Church spread throughout the world. We see the Body of Christ, and it inspires hope and belief in the Head.[22]

Augustine supports this close association between Jesus and His Body, the Church, from the account of Paul's conversion. Jesus interrupts Saul on the road to Damascus, saying, "Saul, Saul, why are you persecuting Me?" Paul replied, "Who are You, Lord?" Jesus then responded, "I am Jesus, whom you are persecuting" (Acts 9:4–5). Saul is persecuting the Church, but because the Church is Christ's Body, Jesus asks Saul, "Why are you persecuting *Me*?" From this passage, it is clear that Jesus sees the Church as part of Himself.

All Tribes and Nations

Christians believe that the Church can never be existentially threatened. Jesus is risen, physically, and His Body the Church will rise too. Our Lord has promised us that no matter how many days, years, or millennia pass before then, on the day that Jesus returns in

---

22   See John 20:24–29, where Jesus appears to Thomas after the resurrection.

triumph, the Church will be here waiting for Him. Sometimes the future of the Church has looked bleak, but she has always survived. This is because God sustains the Church, and He does not fail.

The Church consists of all Christians who have ever lived and will ever live. In Revelation 7:9–10, John describes a vision of the Church Triumphant:

> After this I looked, and behold, a great multitude that no one could number, from every nation, from all tribes and peoples and languages, standing before the throne and before the Lamb, clothed in white robes, with palm branches in their hands, and crying out with a loud voice, "Salvation belongs to our God who sits on the throne, and to the Lamb!"

Revelation can be challenging to understand, with many competing interpretations (and misinterpretations) available. A good way to think about it is a vision of what is happening in heaven on the other side of Jesus' ascension. The "great multitude" in John's vision are the faithful departed—our brothers and sisters in Christ who have died and are now with Jesus in paradise.

Many churches have a Communion rail around the altar in a half circle. There is rich and beautiful symbolism here. In Communion, we both receive Christ's true body and blood and are made to be His Body through the work of the Holy Spirit. We can imagine the half

"Therefore, since we are surrounded by so great a cloud of witnesses, let us also lay aside every weight, and sin which clings so closely, and let us run with endurance the race that is set before us, looking to Jesus, the founder and perfecter of our faith, who for the joy that was set before Him endured the cross, despising the shame, and is seated at the right hand of the throne of God." (Hebrews 12:1–2)

circle as being completed by the saints who are not present—both the faithful departed and our brothers and sisters around the world. The half-circle Communion rail reminds us that when we commune, we partake of the marriage feast of the Lamb. We are participating in something that unites us across time and space to the universal Church.

When I look across the altar from the Communion rail, at some churches I see carvings and images decorating the altar space, reminding me of the saints to whom I am connected in this Sacrament. When I walk back to my seat, I often find myself thinking about my family and friends who live in different states and about Christians all over the world gathering in their local churches and receiving the same body and blood of Christ. In this localized and specific celebration of the Lord's Supper, Jesus unites us to Himself, and we are therefore united also with one another.

The hymn "This Is the Feast," which is part of the Lutheran liturgy, gives voice to this truth:

> **This is the feast of victory for our God. Alleluia.**
> **Sing with all the people of God, and join in the**
> **hymn of all creation:**
> **Blessing and honor and glory and might be to God**
> **and the Lamb forever. Amen.**
> **This is the feast of victory for our God,**
> **for the Lamb who was slain has begun His reign.**
> **Alleluia, alleluia.**[23]

In Genesis, God promised Noah and then Abraham that "all the nations of the earth shall be blessed" through their families (Genesis 26:4). The coming of Jesus fulfilled that promise, and the Church is the result. We are now, as the Church, "all the nations

---

23   *LSB*, p. 171–72. The text of this hymn is derived from Revelation 5 and 19.

of the earth" that are blessed because of the Messiah, foretold in Genesis and fulfilled in Jesus, who will finally return as promised in Revelation.

Division in the Church

T he Church united throughout all the world from the beginning of time until Christ returns is a stirring and hopeful image. It is how Jesus sees us as the Church! But I'm guessing that while you may see this vision of the Church in Scripture and like the idea of it, it may not resonate very well with your actual *experiences* of churches and Christians.

The reality is that the Church does not appear to be united. There are different denominations—different divisions, traditions, and church structures—and they all believe different things about Jesus, the Church, and the teachings of Scripture. We don't like these divisions. They sow seeds of doubt in our minds, making us wonder: If all these churches can't agree, is the basic message of Christianity certain or knowable? Do divisions mean that this whole thing isn't true? Why do theologians fight so much? Why can't we all just recognize that we love Jesus and get along?

Divisions in the Church are not new. Paul spoke in the New Testament about divisions among the faithful. Disagreement in the Body of Christ saddened Paul as well. He says in two of his letters:

> I appeal to you, brothers, to watch out for those who cause divisions and create obstacles contrary to the doctrine that you have been taught; avoid them. For such persons do not serve our Lord Christ, but their own appetites, and by smooth talk and flattery they deceive the hearts of the naive. (Romans 16:17–18)

> **I appeal to you, brothers, by the name of our Lord Jesus
> Christ, that all of you agree, and that there be no divi-
> sions among you, but that you be united in the same
> mind and the same judgment.** (1 Corinthians 1:10)

God's Word instructs us to be united, but this unity is not meant to be superficial. We are called to be united in doctrine. Paul appeals to the readers to avoid any false teachers who "create obstacles contrary to the doctrine that you have been taught" and to be "united in the same mind and the same judgment." Paul does not make light of doctrinal disagreements; he wants us to be united, yes, but united in the profession of the rule of faith.

These verses clearly show that division is not good. However, Paul also says, "For, in the first place, when you come together as a church, I hear that there are divisions among you. And I believe it in part, for there must be factions among you in order that those who are genuine among you may be recognized" (1 Corinthians 11:18–19). When we insist on unity in the Church to the extent that we do not allow discussion about the truths of Scripture, we prevent "those who are genuine" among us from being recognized.

The Reformation era provides a classic example. Luther and his fellow reformers sought to have a conversation with the pope and bishops of the Church about theological matters that they thought the church leadership was getting wrong. Instead of discussing in good faith, the Roman Church attempted to suppress the reformers' concerns. When Luther refused to recant his writings because he did not see how they had violated Scripture, Pope Leo X excommunicated him. This forced the Reformation Church to operate outside of the institutional structure of the Roman Church—something they did not intend to do when they set out to have theological discussions.

As a Protestant, I have often heard the accusation that Luther opened the door to modern denominationalism by sowing seeds of dissension in Christendom. This was not Luther's intent and is an unfair recounting of his legacy.[24] He took the teachings of the Church seriously, which meant examining them to see how they aligned with Scripture and correcting them where necessary.

We tend to think the Ancient Church was more unified than the Church is today, and perhaps it was. But the Church Fathers of the third and fourth centuries struggled with unity in the Church as well. As discussed in previous chapters, the Arian heresy caused much division in the Church. Basil of Caesarea, a bishop and teacher during that time, expressed concern for the faith of the individual Christian in times of schism. He wrote:

> I will yield to none in my earnest wish and prayer to see the day when those who are one in sentiment shall all fill the same assembly. Indeed it would be monstrous to feel pleasure in the schisms and divisions of the Churches, and not to consider that the greatest of goods consists in the knitting together of the members of Christ's body.[25]

Basil desired peace and harmony in the Church specifically because he thought this would be best for the faith of individual believers. He recognized that divisions in the Church hurt our individual faith, either by fracturing relationships or by sowing doubt about the true doctrine of the Church. However, he did not seek unity at all costs. During the Arian controversy, when he believed the theological truths of the faith were at stake, he suggested it would be more faithful for true Christians to worship in the desert than in a church building with heretics.

---

24   One could just as easily assert that it was Pope Leo X that caused denominationalism by excommunicating Luther instead of engaging him in a good-faith conversation about the theological issues at hand.

25   Basil of Caesarea, Letter CLVI, in *St. Basil: Letters and Select Works*, ed. Philip Schaff and Henry Wace, A Select Library of the Nicene and Post-Nicene Fathers of the Christian Church, second series, vol. 8 (New York: Christian Literature Company, 1895), 210–11.

Our own experiences in Christian communities may convince us that Basil was correct: division in the Church is hard on our faith as individuals. But Basil was also not so afraid of schism that he compromised the Creed. Basil recognized that the rule of faith is central, and he was willing to risk schism for the sake of doctrinal purity. Many Christians today feel as Basil did—that divisions are sad and detrimental, but necessary when the truths of Scripture are on the line.

However, there are others who find theological differences unimportant. Many churches today are no longer concerned about the authority of Scripture or the right view of the Sacraments. Progressive church bodies seek to sweep the "historical baggage" under the rug and join together in being good, well-meaning people who love the world for the sake of Jesus, all while downplaying the teachings of Jesus. These churches either ignore or seek to eliminate divisions in the name of ecumenism (that is, the appearance of unity), or they show no concern over the existing divides.

Divisions Exist Because of Sin

Hidden just beneath the surface of all division is the presence of sin. We fail to agree with one another because the truth is not obvious to us. Politically, personally, theologically—people disagree, sometimes vehemently! This reveals two things: humans are not omniscient, and our ability to reason is fallible.

Juxtaposed with our own shortcomings is the truth that is Jesus Christ, the Word made flesh for us. God's knowledge is the opposite of our own imperfect understanding. He does know everything, and His reasoning is flawless. God is beyond our comprehension. He gave us His infallible Word precisely because we could never hope to know anything about Him with certainty if we had to rely on our own abilities or discernment.

I know I am not alone in finding it deeply uncomfortable when family members or friends are on different sides of important truth claims about the reality of the world. When there is something important to be known, and it is obvious that at least one person in the relationship does not know it, relationships feel less secure. This points us to our own sin and imperfection—hence the discomfort. We may believe that we are right, but we grieve that our friend or loved one is wrong. If we are not certain about our views, this uncertainty can cause us to grieve our own frailty. Some of us may suppress this grief with anger or hostility. However we react, disagreement confronts us with our own inadequacy.

Not everyone has these strong feelings about disagreement. Modern culture offers another option: ambivalence or denying the reality of objective truth. If there is no such thing as truth, then no one has to be wrong. If no one is wrong, maybe none of us are broken, fallible, or sinful. Perhaps we can sidestep this discomfort and grief with a breezy, "That's cool if that works for you. That's not my truth, but whatever floats your boat."

> In the Small Catechism, the explanation of the Third Article of the Creed begins, "I believe that I cannot by my own reason or strength believe in Jesus Christ, my Lord, or come to Him." We read in 1 Corinthians 2:14 that "the natural person does not accept the things of the Spirit of God, for they are folly to him, and he is not able to understand them because they are spiritually discerned." Scripture teaches that our ability to understand the things of God was lost in the fall. To understand God's Word, we need His Holy Spirit.

However, we cannot remain neutral or ambivalent for long. If we reject the absolute truth passed down to us, we must eventually create a new one to replace it. Our society's new "truth" seems to be that your beliefs are wrong if they place any limits on others' ability to do what they want or live how they want. Progressive Christianity has fallen victim to this new truth claim and has set aside the rule of faith to make room for it. Because these churches ignore or reject the concept of sin, divisions do not bother them. However, for conservative traditions that hold a high view of Scripture, division is always sad, even as it is inevitable.

Divisions exist within the Church because it is made up of sinners. This is why Paul says we need divisions, in a sense (see 1 Corinthians 11:18–19). Because we are sinful, our leaders and authority structures will get it wrong at times. Because we are not omniscient, our reason and ability to interpret Scripture on our own will fail us. Because we are not always Christlike, feelings will be hurt, personalities will not always mesh, and disagreements will sometimes become personal and heated. If it were up to us to unite the Church and keep her unified, we would be in serious trouble. Thankfully, this is not our job.

Unity in Christ

When I was learning to drive, my driving instructors and my parents told me to aim high. If I was worried about staying in my lane and not hitting the other cars, it didn't help to watch the lane markers or look at the other cars. By looking high up the road toward my goal, I was able to drive straight and do so without hitting anyone else. In one sense, unity in the Church is like that. We cannot achieve unity by worrying about every little thing every other church body is doing. We do not become more like Christ by trying to become more like one another.

Instead, we aim high by focusing on our Savior. The Church may appear fragmented and broken to our eyes, but the truth is that she is united in and by Jesus Christ. Christians become unified not by trying hard to unite with one another but by being united to Christ.

Jesus unites us to Himself. Because we are each united with Him, we are one with our fellow Christians too. This is a spiritual reality now, but it will be fully realized in the life to come, when sin no longer breaks what should be whole. Through our eyes, we see the division and imperfections of the Church, but when we look through Jesus' eyes, we can see her unity in Him.

First Peter 3:20–21 compares Baptism to the ark that preserved Noah and his family through the flood. In the arms of the Church, we are as safe and secure from judgment as Noah and his family were from the waters of the flood. Being part of the Church is intrinsically connected with our hope in the life to come. Belonging to the Body should offer immense comfort, safety, and rootedness in God's plan. Different church bodies attempt to point us to this reality in various ways, hoping to provide that comfort and assurance to each Christian.

Most church bodies fall into one of two categories: asking you either to place your trust in institutional authorities made up of men or to look within yourself for this comfort and certainty. For example, in the Roman Catholic tradition, the magisterium of the church has the authority to determine who is part of the church and who is not. In many Evangelical traditions, someone becomes a member of the church by making a decision to believe in Jesus and follow Him. Some churches emphasize looking for the fruit of repentance and faith in the lives of believers to provide comfort and certainty in their salvation. This also falls into those two categories: you trust your own perceptions of whether your fruit is "good enough," or you trust authority figures in your church body to tell you if someone is "yielding good fruit." Either way, the believer's status as part of the church is up to human interpretation.

It is hard to find comfort and assurance based only on human interpretation. We need something objective, outside of our own weak abilities and anxieties, something that is not man-made.

The Lutheran teaching of the marks of the Church (discussed in chapter 2) provides this. We point not to human structures nor to the individual heart of the believer, but to Christ and the specific ways He has promised to unite us to Himself and make us one in Him. Instead of finding comfort in the man-made forms that our churches take, we find comfort in those marks that are instituted by Christ. Jesus gives us His Word and His Sacraments to unite us to Himself. When we receive the Lord's Supper or hear the Gospel preached, we know we are within the safety of the ark of the Church.

Unity cannot be forced, lied about, or pretended. Unity either exists or it does not. Even if we could do away with all the institutional and denominational lines today, we could not eliminate our own sin. We could not create in every believer a heart and mind that fully understands and accepts the entirety of God's truth. We could not comfort every conscience just by doing all things the same everywhere. But these desires we have—for no divisions, for a heart and mind that accepts God's truth, for a comforted conscience—will be met when Christ returns.

In our view now, unity in the Church may seem imperfect or wishful. But we see only in part. The unified Church that we long for, we will get! Until that day, we place our hope not in what the Church looks like on the outside but in the reality to come and in what Jesus is doing in and through her for us by the power of the Holy Spirit.

The Hope of the Church

F rom her beginning, the Church has grappled with division and doctrinal disagreement. The New Testament Epistles were written to correct errors and to point churches to greater faithfulness. They still serve this purpose today. Paul speaks of division in the Church as unfortunate and something to avoid because it means that someone is misunderstanding Scripture; division points to doctrinal error. Errors in teaching deprive believers of true comfort in Christ and the hope of the life to come.

The hope of the Church is in the life to come, the promised restoration of all things when Christ returns, and the guarantee of life forever with God. On the Last Day, we will truly be united. We will be of one mind, as one body, unified in Christ. This is the Gospel—that our sin, division, and broken relationships, both with God and with one another, will be washed clean by the blood of Christ and that Jesus will present His Bride to Himself "without spot or wrinkle or any such thing" (Ephesians 5:27). We know this day will come, but in the meantime, we find our hope not in false unity that is forced or a mere pretense to avoid conflict but in the true unity that comes from our shared identity as the Body of Christ.

Because the unity of the Church is part of our eschatological hope, we must take it seriously. On the one hand, we should not be argumentative, drawing lines where God's Word does not do so. On the other hand, Jesus Himself is the Word made flesh (see John 1). Jesus' words cannot be separated from Him. He and His Word are one. Therefore, disagreement about issues such as justification (how we are brought into a right relationship with God), the atonement (what Jesus' death on the cross accomplishes for us), the Sacraments, and how

> Luther's Small Catechism states and explains the Eighth Commandment this way: "You shall not give false testimony against your neighbor. What does this mean? We should fear and love God so that we do not tell lies about our neighbor, betray him, slander him, or hurt his reputation, but defend him, speak well of him, and explain everything in the kindest way." Naturally, when speaking about our brothers and sisters in Christ, either in our own or in other church traditions, we should strive to speak well of them whenever possible.

we receive faith are important because they are about the character of our Lord—who Jesus has revealed Himself to be.

At times of confession in Church history, faithful Christians have been persecuted, both by unbelievers and by the religious authorities of their day, for the sake of the Gospel. When we attempt to gloss over the theological differences that underlie various church traditions, how humbling it is to remember that our brothers and sisters in Christ were willing to die for some of those doctrines! Rather than make light of important doctrinal differences, we should love one another, striving for unity in all areas where we do agree and "explaining everything in the kindest way" when we do not.

If theological differences are ultimately differences of belief about the character of our Lord, or about the person and work of Jesus, we could say that Christians in other faith traditions know Jesus, but perhaps they don't agree about who He is or what He says He has done for us. You can know people, trust them, and have a good relationship with them and still be wrong in your understanding of how they think or who they are. When we profess that we believe these specific tenets of faith regarding the person and work of Christ, it does not mean that we believe that Christians who disagree with us have no relationship with Jesus.

As a parent, I do not think that my young children necessarily "get me" or understand what makes me tick. They don't even understand my words to them all the time. Sometimes they understand what I'm saying but disagree and pretend they don't hear me. Our relationship with Jesus can be like that. Disagreement over theological matters is important because it is about our Savior. We should want to know Him better, to know His Word well, and to understand who He has revealed Himself to be. In this, just as I work with my children to help them grow in maturity and knowledge, we should also strive to mature in our faith so that we may have more true unity in our understanding of Christ's work for us.

Our Unity Is Greater than Our Division

· · · · · · · · · · · · · · · · · ·

I'd like to offer two points of encouragement about division within the Church.

First, try to zoom out. Up close, denominational lines may look like an impossible number of fractures that destroy the integrity of the whole. But when we look at the totality of Church history, the Church's confession has been remarkably consistent despite two thousand years of political and cultural change. Christians who profess the faith of the Apostles' Creed have existed since Pentecost throughout the entire world. Even denominations that do not use a creed liturgically would likely acknowledge the historical veracity of the Creed's content. While the theological distinctions between denominations are significant, and certainly it is impossible that all traditions are correct as they do contradict one another, the Church still gives a strong, universal witness to the life, death, and resurrection of Jesus Christ and the atonement He made for the sins of the world. This level of agreement should never be downplayed! There truly is a universal Church, and all Christians can draw comfort from this fact.

Second, the doctrinal distinctives of each theological tradition point to the importance of the rule of faith. Christians across denominational lines tend to agree that doctrinal differences matter. Roman Catholics, Eastern Orthodox, Lutherans, Anglicans, Baptists, Pentecostals, and so on all realize that their distinctive teachings color their body of doctrine as a whole—hence they refuse to compromise on such significant issues as the nature of the Word and Sacraments that mark their churches. While the existence of these differences are a sign of our sinful imperfections, the high regard in which we hold our theology is a witness to its importance. Jesus Himself is the Word who was made flesh. Our professed theology is what we believe about the character of our Savior, which is why the Church cannot compromise on the details of her theology.

In Isaiah 9:6–7, the promised Messiah is called the Prince of Peace. We are promised that "of the increase of His government and of peace there will be no end." But in Luke 12, Jesus speaks about the kind of peace that He will bring as Messiah, and it is not what we might expect:

> **Do you think that I have come to give peace on earth?**
> **No, I tell you, but rather division. For from now on**
> **in one house there will be five divided, three against**
> **two and two against three. They will be divided, father**
> **against son and son against father, mother against**
> **daughter and daughter against mother, mother-in-**
> **law against her daughter-in-law and daughter-in-law**
> **against mother-in-law. (Luke 12:51–53)**

The peace that Jesus will bring is not the peace of complete intellectual agreement. It is something more real than that, more lasting than that, and more eternal. It exists only imperfectly now, but one day it will exist in perfection.

Final Thought
· · · · · · · · · · · ·

*T*he Church is bigger than our local congregation. It is the fellowship of the saints united in Christ across time and space. On the final day, we will witness the multitude that no one can count—the Body of Christ. The Church is both the means by which we encounter God and an expression of our collective hope. Because of sin, the Church today is divided. Our inability to know the truth perfectly leads to theological disagreements and interpersonal conflict in the Body of Christ. As sinners, we cannot create true unity in the Church by our own reason or power. But Jesus is using the Church, imperfect though she may be, to draw us to Himself. It is Jesus' job to unite the Church, and He promises to do so. He does so now through His Word and Sacraments and will do so ultimately in the new creation. Jesus sees the Church as a timeless entity spread throughout the whole world.

Discussion Questions

· ·

1. What are some of the ways you have seen division hurt the Church? This could be on a local level in your community or on a global level when considering denominational divides. Have you been hurt personally by divisiveness in the Church?

2. Read Philippians 2:1–18. How does Paul describe the Church? How does he instruct the Christians in Philippi to behave? What does this passage teach us about unity and division in the Body of Christ?

3. Each of the following texts talks about divisions in the Church. Take some time to look these up and see what the connection is between division and the pure teaching of the Word.

   - Romans 16:17–18
   - 1 Corinthians 1:10
   - 1 Corinthians 11:18–19
   - 1 Corinthians 12:25
   - Galatians 5:20
   - Titus 3:9–10
   - Jude 19

4. Have you ever been tempted to express a false unity for the sake of avoiding conflict? In light of the Scripture you've read, what do you think is the proper balance between living in peace despite disagreement and speaking the truth in love? Is conflict always bad? When is it necessary?

Heavenly Father, thank You for loving the whole world so much that You sent Your Son. Thank You for Your promise to make all things new. Thank You that Your plan of redemption is big enough for everyone and that no one is outside the reach of Your love. Our hearts long for the unity and peace that is to come when Jesus returns. Forgive us for the times when we have tried to force that unity by compromising on Your truth or by ignoring our own sin. Forgive us for loving the idea of peace more than the One who brings peace. Send Your Spirit to work peace and trust in You in each of our hearts so that the Church on earth today may better reflect the unity that is to come. In Jesus' name we pray. Amen.

PART II

Jesus' Gifts to the Church

. . . .

WHAT THE CHURCH DOES

I n part I, we introduced Tertullian's three-part definition of the Church—summarized as *creed*, *practice*, and *eschatological hope*—and explored how Jesus sees the Church in conjunction with each of these components. We learned about the centrality of the Word of God in the Church, the sanctifying work of the Holy Spirit through the Church, and the universal nature of the Church as a people throughout time and space united by our hope in the life to come.

In part II, we will revisit each of these components on a more tangible level. Our God is not a God of distant philosophies or mere spiritual truths. He is a God of the concrete, of the created, of the objective, and of the *real*. Jesus has given His Church gifts that connect us to Him and build us up as His Body. Each remaining chapter explores one of these gifts Christ has instituted for us.

Chapter 5 discusses the pastoral office—a role instituted in Scripture to provide the Word of God to His people and to administer the Sacraments on behalf of His people. The pastoral office is the teaching office of the Church and is given to us to safeguard the creed, or rule of faith.

In chapter 6, we will study the Sacraments and the way that faith is worked and strengthened in the hearts of believers through Baptism and the Lord's Supper. Gathering together around God's Word and Sacraments is the practice of the faithful that is given to the Church to help us grow in our faith.

In chapter 7, we will look at Jesus' final instructions to His disciples before His ascension: "Go therefore and make disciples of all nations" (Matthew 28:19). We will see how the Church's evangelistic impulse is a natural outpouring of the work the Holy Spirit is doing in and through each of us, and how it is the ultimate expression of our eschatological hope in Christ.

Finally, chapter 8 will conclude with our roles as individuals in the Body of Christ.

Authority and the Pastoral Office

....

MARTIN LUTHER

Martin Luther is best known for the instigating role he played in the Protestant Reformation. He lived from 1483 to 1546 in Germany, and his nailing of the Ninety-Five Theses to the church door in Wittenberg was a catalyst for the Reformation. Luther was a central figure in rediscovering the theology of the Bible. He called on church authorities to stop practices that had arisen in the Medieval Church that were contrary to Scripture. He is also known for translating the Bible into German for the first time and for writing Luther's Small and Large Catechisms, as well as many other theological works. The Lutheran Church is named for him, as his name came to represent his teachings, and Lutherans believe that the teachings of Luther and the other reformers in his tradition are not only the teachings of Scripture but also the teachings of historic Christianity.

It may seem counterintuitive to start a chapter on the gift of Church authority by highlighting a man so often accused of usurping Church authority and fracturing the Western Church. However, Luther was not motivated by ambivalence about Church unity or a desire to usurp authority (as discussed in chapter 4). In fact, Luther had a very high view of authority. He believed that authority figures on earth derive their authority from God and reflect His care and provision for His people.

Luther makes this clear in his teaching on the Fourth Commandment in the Large Catechism, where he describes the honor due to parents and then extends that honor to all other authority figures, both in the government and in the Church. He clarifies that he does not mean that we are to honor any person who claims authority but only those who hold offices instituted by God and who rightly image God's care and provision to His people: "Besides these there are still spiritual fathers. They are not like those in the papacy, who have had themselves called fathers but have performed no function of the fatherly office [Matthew 23:9]. For the only ones called spiritual fathers are those who govern and guide us by God's Word."[26] Luther holds those in authority to a standard outside of and above themselves. They are to execute their divinely ordained office according to God's Word and not according to their own preferences.

This is a selection from the Smalcald Articles, written by Luther in 1537 when he was gravely ill and thought he was dying. He recovered and lived for another decade, but at the time, he desired to clarify his own beliefs, as people were already trying to invoke his name and assign views to him that he did not hold. This excerpt presents Luther's understanding of the authority of the Church and the pastoral office.

---

26   Large Catechism I 158.

The Keys are an office and power given by Christ to the Church for binding and loosing sin [Matthew 16:19]. This applies not only to gross and well-known sins, but also the subtle, hidden sins that are known only to God. As it is written, "Who can discern his errors?" (Psalm 19:12). And St. Paul himself complains that "with my flesh I serve the law of sin" (Romans 7:25). It is not in our power to judge which, how great, and how many the sins are. This belongs to God alone. As it is written, "Enter not into judgment with your servant, for no one living is righteous before you" (Psalm 143:2). Paul says, "I am not aware of anything against myself, but I am not thereby acquitted" (1 Corinthians 4:4).

Absolution, or the Power of the Keys, is an aid against sin and a consolation for a bad conscience; it is ordained by Christ in the Gospel [Matthew 16:19]. Therefore, Confession and Absolution should by no means be abolished in the Church. This is especially for the sake of timid consciences and untrained young people, so they may be examined and instructed in Christian doctrine. But the listing of sins should be free to everyone, as to what a person wishes to list or not to list. For as long as we are in the flesh, we will not lie when we say, "I am a poor man, full of sin"; "I see in my members another law"; and such (Romans 7:23). Since private Absolution originates in the Office of the Keys, it should not be despised, but greatly and highly esteemed, along with all other offices of the Christian Church. In issues relating to the spoken, outward Word, we must firmly hold that God grants His Spirit or grace to no one except through or with the preceding outward Word [Galatians 3:2, 5]. This protects us from the enthusiasts (i.e., souls who boast that they have the Spirit without and before the Word). They judge Scripture or the spoken Word and explain and stretch it at their pleasure, as Münzer did. Many still do this today, wanting to be sharp judges between the Spirit and the letter, and yet they do not know what they are saying [2 Corinthians 3:6]. Actually, the papacy too is nothing but sheer enthusiasm. The pope boasts that all rights exist in the shrine of his heart. Whatever he decides and commands within his church is from the Spirit and is right, even though it is above and contrary to Scripture and the spoken Word. . . .

If the bishops would be true bishops and would devote themselves to the Church and the Gospel, we might grant them to ordain and confirm us and our preachers. This would be for the sake of love and unity, but not because it was necessary. However, they would have to give up all comedies and spectacular display of unchristian parade and pomp. But they do not even want to be true bishops, but worldly lords and princes, who will neither preach, nor teach, nor baptize, nor administer the Lord's Supper, nor perform any work or office of the Church. Furthermore; they persecute and condemn those who do discharge these functions, having been called to do so. So the Church should not be deprived of ministers because of the bishops. Therefore, as the ancient examples of the Church and the fathers teach us, we ourselves should ordain suitable persons to this office. Even according to their own laws, they do not have the right to forbid or prevent us. For their laws say that those ordained even by heretics are truly ordained and stay ordained.

As St. Jerome writes of the Church at Alexandria, at first it was governed in common by priests and preachers, without bishops. . . .

We do not agree with them that they[27] are the Church. They are not the Church. Nor will we listen to those things that, under the name of Church, they command or forbid. Thank God, ‹today› a seven-year-old child knows what the Church is, namely, the holy believers and lambs who hear the voice of their Shepherd [John 10:11–16]. For the children pray, "I believe in one holy Christian Church." This holiness does not come from albs, tonsures, long gowns, and other ceremonies they made up without Holy Scripture, but from God's Word and true faith.[28]

Here Luther describes the connection between the Keys (absolution), good order, and Church authority. He understands that God's purpose in giving all these gifts to the Church is to comfort consciences. Jesus died on the cross so that the sins of all may be forgiven. This is the central message of the Church, and the pastor's job is to deliver that forgiveness to God's people. It is wrong to withhold God's forgiveness from those who are repentant or to place obstacles between a sincere believer and their complete forgiveness, as the practices of the medieval Catholic Church clearly did. Luther uses sharp words here against those who misuse their authority, but he does so because of his heart for those who need to hear God's forgiveness.

---

27 Luther is addressing the pope and leaders of the Roman Catholic Church here. He challenges their assertion that they are the Church because they are not preaching God's Word.

28 Smalcald Articles, part, III, articles VII, VIII, X, XII.

Matthew 16 and
the Office of the Keys

. . . .

*I*n the excerpt from the Smalcald Articles, Luther explained the Office of the Keys. The Office (or Power) of the Keys is the authority that Jesus has given the Church to forgive the sins of those who are repentant and to not forgive the sins of the unrepentant. When we consider Church authority, we inevitably study Matthew 16, in which Jesus institutes that authority. An additional, practical reason to explore this text is because the Roman Catholic Church uses it as the primary scriptural support for their doctrine of the papacy. With so many Christians leaning on this passage to understand what it means to be the Church, we must give it proper consideration.

> "And when He had said this, He breathed on them and said to them, 'Receive the Holy Spirit. If you forgive the sins of any, they are forgiven them; if you withhold forgiveness from any, it is withheld.'"
> (John 20:22–23)

In Matthew 16, Jesus asks Peter, "Who do you say that I am?" Peter replies, "You are the Christ, the Son of the living God" (vv. 15–16). Jesus responds:

> Blessed are you, Simon Bar-Jonah! For flesh and blood has not revealed this to you, but My Father who is in heaven. And I tell you, you are Peter, and on this rock I will build My church, and the gates of hell shall not prevail against it. I will give you the keys of the kingdom of heaven, and whatever you bind on earth shall be bound in heaven, and whatever you loose on earth shall be loosed in heaven. (vv. 17–19)

What comfort Jesus provides here—not even the gates of hell can prevail against the Church Jesus builds! Unfortunately, the controversy over the interpretation of the passage has, at times, drawn our focus from this assurance. The Roman Catholic Church has traditionally interpreted this text to support the institution of the papacy; they take Jesus' words to mean that Peter himself is the rock on whom the Church is built. The Protestant view is that the rock upon which the Church is built refers to Peter's confession that Jesus is the Christ. Which is correct? To determine that, we turn to the original language of the passage.

In his commentary on Matthew, Jeffrey Gibbs analyzes the Greek grammar of this passage. Because Jesus uses the Greek singular *you* in verses 17–19, Gibbs notes that it would be disingenuous to completely separate Peter from the rock on which the Church is to be built. The text links Peter's making this statement with Jesus' assertion that this is the rock upon which the Church will be built. The Church is built not only on the content of Peter's confession, but also on the act of confessing—that is, on the ministry of the apostles in preaching this confession. While Jesus is speaking to Peter in verses 17–19, this is part of a larger conversation between Jesus and all twelve disciples. In verse 15, when Jesus says, "Who do you say that I am?" the "you" is plural. And in verse 20, Jesus charges all the disciples to tell no one He is the Christ.[29] To summarize, the rock upon which the Church is built is not Peter, but it is also not merely the statement, "You are the Christ." The foundation of the Church is the preaching ministry that declares this truth, just as Peter did in the passage.

In the Treatise on the Power and Primacy of the Pope, Philip Melanchthon understands Matthew 16 in this way. He also demonstrates that Church Fathers of the first several centuries did

---

29   Jeffrey Gibbs, *Matthew 11:2–20:34*, Concordia Commentary (St. Louis: Concordia Publishing House, 2010), 818–19.

The Treatise on the Power and Primacy of the Pope is one of the confessional documents included in the Book of Concord. It was written at the same time as the Smalcald Articles to further clarify the Lutheran position on the papacy and Church authority. Look it up for a more thorough examination of this topic.

not interpret this text to support an institution or office such as the papacy.

As for the declaration "on this rock I will build My church" [Matthew 16:18], certainly the Church has not been built upon the authority of a man. Rather, it has been built upon the ministry of the confession Peter made, in which he proclaims that Jesus is the Christ, the Son of God [Matthew 16:16]. Therefore, Christ addresses Peter as a minister, "On this rock," that is, this ministry. Therefore, He addresses him as a minister of this office in which this confession, and doctrine is to be in operation and says: "Upon this rock," i.e., this preaching and preaching office. . . .

Most of the holy Church Fathers, such as Origen, Cyprian, Augustine, Hilary, and Bede, interpret the passage "on this rock" in this way, as not referring to the person of Peter. Chrysostom says this: "Upon this rock," not upon Peter. For He built His Church not upon man, but upon the faith of Peter. But what was his faith? "You are the Christ, the Son of the living God." Hilary says: The Father revealed to Peter that he should say, "You are the Son of the living God" [Matthew 16:17]. Therefore, the building of the Church is upon this rock of confession. This faith is the foundation of the Church.[30]

---

30   Treatise on the Power and Primacy of the Pope, 25, 27–29.

In Matthew 16, Jesus institutes the Office of Public Ministry. Here He tells His disciples that the Church will be built upon their confession of faith in Him. He also makes two big promises: He promises that the gates of hell will not prevail against His Church, and He promises that sins will be forgiven in His name through the Office of Public Ministry. This passage certainly indicates that divine authority is given to the Church and, specifically within the Church, to the pastoral office.

The medieval papacy is a classic example of abusive and exploitative authority structures, but it is not the only time when the gift of authority has been misused in churches to great harm. I know many friends, family members, and acquaintances who have been hurt by people or ideas within the Church that weaponized this authority to exert power and control in ways that can only be described as abusive. It is always considered abuse when a pastor misuses his authority. After an incident of pastoral misconduct, it is all but guaranteed that the congregation the pastor served will be deeply hurt. People will lose their faith and leave their church. The congregation may not recover their trust in the pastoral office for decades, and future pastors will struggle to lead those who have been hurt in the past.

Godly authority stands in sharp contrast to this kind of abusive authority. Jesus approaches His Church with absolute authority, yes, but also with gentleness and service. Authority is intended to be a gift of God for the benefit of those under it. Wives are submissive to their husbands. Children are to honor their parents. Citizens honor their governing authorities. Parishioners are to respect their pastors. And those in authority are to serve selflessly, using their authority to care for and love those God has entrusted to them.

Part of our difficulty with institutions comes from our own sinful relationship with authority. Sin taints all authority relationships. We see this from the moment after the fall in Genesis 3, when God says to Eve, "Your desire shall be contrary to your husband, but he shall rule over you" (v. 16). In our fallen world, those with authority often sinfully exploit and misuse it, and those under authority sinfully fight against it and desire to be their own authority. In both cases, this is idolatry—it reveals our desire to be our own god.

The pastor's role is to image Christ to the congregation, and when a pastor does this poorly, people struggle to see Christ's loving nature, as we would expect. This is why in James 3:1 we read that "not many of you should become teachers, my brothers, for you know that we who teach will be judged with greater strictness." This role is intended to be a gift to God's people, so God's people steward it carefully. The role is not designed to elevate the person occupying it. Rather, the office of pastor as instituted by Jesus is all about imaging Jesus' love and servant-leadership to His Bride, the Church.

The Vocation of Pastor

One of the most straightforward texts discussing the qualifications for the pastoral office is 1 Timothy 3, in which Paul gives instructions to a young pastor on how best to lead his congregation. When we examine the scriptural criteria for pastoral ministry, we don't just see the guidelines for who can and cannot be a pastor. That is definitely there, and it's very useful to have! But as you read this passage, think about what these criteria teach us about the office of pastor itself. What does the pastor do? What role does he fill in the life of the Church?

> If anyone aspires to the office of overseer, he desires a
> noble task. Therefore an overseer must be above
> reproach, the husband of one wife, sober-minded,
> self-controlled, respectable, hospitable, able to teach,
> not a drunkard, not violent but gentle, not quarrel-
> some, not a lover of money. He must manage his own
> household well, with all dignity keeping his children

submissive, for if someone does not know how to manage his own household, how will he care for God's church? He must not be a recent convert, or he may become puffed up with conceit and fall into the condemnation of the devil. Moreover, he must be well thought of by outsiders, so that he may not fall into disgrace, into a snare of the devil. (1 Timothy 3:1–7)

Pastors are called by the congregation from among the faithful to publicly proclaim the Word of God, to administer the Sacraments, and to declare the forgiveness of sins. When a pastor lapses in a significant way, whether by abusing his office or by demonstrating a lack of judgment or godliness in his personal life, spiritual damage is done to his

> In the New Testament, the words *overseer*, *bishop*, and *elder* are all used synonymously to refer to the pastoral office. As time went on, these words took on more specific meanings. When we read Paul, though, it is helpful to know that these terms all refer to the same position: the Office of Public Ministry.

congregation. It is hurtful in much the same way that any of these deficiencies in a parent hurts the children he or she is raising. This is why Paul says in verses 4–5 that a pastor must manage his own household well. We live in a world that does not like to acknowledge sin, but as uncomfortable as it may be to admit, we all recognize that children are best served by parents who are married to each other, sober minded, self-controlled, respectable, not drunkards, not violent, and the like. In other words, the presence of significant unrepented sin in a person's life means that he or she cannot image God's benevolent and loving authority well to those under his or her authority. Parents image God's love and care to their children and are given to them for this purpose, which is why it is so damaging when they do not fill this role with integrity. Similarly, pastors who do not fill this role with integrity will hurt their congregation.

Beyond the character qualifications, a pastor should also be "hospitable" and "able to teach" (v. 2). By being a man of good character, the pastor implicitly teaches us about God's love and care for His flock. By being a man who is able to teach and is hospitable, the pastor explicitly teaches God's Word accurately and well. Each pastor obviously has different skills and giftings, which is a good thing for the Church as a whole. But all pastors should be able both to live out their faith and to articulate their faith clearly so that all of God's people can know Him better.

In verses 6–7, Paul concludes his list of criteria with "not be a recent convert" and "well thought of by outsiders." Paul says in verse 1 that "if anyone aspires to the office of overseer, he desires a noble task," but he tempers that here. He cautions that not just any individual swept up by desire to fill this role is truly qualified. This role is not about fulfilling our own heart's desires but about imaging God to His people. As Jesus told His disciples:

> You know that the rulers of the Gentiles lord it over
> them, and their great ones exercise authority over
> them. It shall not be so among you. But whoever would
> be great among you must be your servant, and who-
> ever would be first among you must be your slave,
> even as the Son of Man came not to be served but
> to serve, and to give His life as a ransom for many.
> (Matthew 20:25–28)

Paul goes on to state his reason for writing this particular letter to Timothy: "I hope to come to you soon, but I am writing these things to you so that, if I delay, you may know how one ought to behave in the household of God, which is the church of the living God, a pillar and buttress of the truth" (1 Timothy 3:14–15).

The Church is the "pillar and buttress of the truth" because it possesses the Word of God, and Paul is saying that, as pastor, Timothy's behavior should reflect this. The role of the pastor, then, is explicitly confirmed in Scripture as a role that guards the rule of faith against heresy and misuse.

In chapter 4, Paul reminds Timothy of his ordination into this office and reinforces what he is to do as pastor:

> Let no one despise you for your youth, but set the believers an example in speech, in conduct, in love, in faith, in purity. Until I come, devote yourself to the public reading of Scripture, to exhortation, to teaching. Do not neglect the gift you have, which was given you by prophecy when the council of elders laid their hands on you. Practice these things, immerse yourself in them, so that all may see your progress. Keep a close watch on yourself and on the teaching. Persist in this, for by so doing you will save both yourself and your hearers. (vv. 12–16)

The laying on of hands by the council of elders in these verses refers to ordination, which Timothy is to consider as a gift and privilege. Pastors are to be devoted to the public reading and teaching of Scripture: they are to set an example to the other believers. Paul's final words, "by so doing you will save both yourself and your hearers," remind us of the importance of the pastor's role. The Word of God has the power to save, and the pastoral office is a gift to the Church for the purpose of declaring the Word to God's people.

Being a pastor is a beautiful yet weighty responsibility. When I read this passage, I feel a sense of respect for the men who take on this calling. I am grateful to God for the gift of pastors and to the pastors in my life for their selfless modeling of what it means to live a life centered around God's Word. This passage encourages us to respect the office of the pastor as a gift from God. As pastors fill that role, setting "an example in speech, in conduct, in love, in faith, in purity" (v. 12), we submit to our Lord by allowing our pastor to lead us in and through God's Word.

The Challenge
of Church Structures

. . . .

S cripture is silent when it comes to church governance at the global level. The only official role we see given to the Church in Scripture is the pastoral office, yet the Church in Scripture is clearly a universal entity. Historically, we can see this sense of unity in the copious exchanging of letters in the Early Church. In the first centuries of Christianity, churches wrote to one another constantly, verifying what they were teaching, sharing lists of their bishops and pastors, and discussing theological controversies. They would not have done this if they had not been deeply aware that the Church is to be united as one. The New Testament Epistles also demonstrate this awareness.

The Church has seen many ecclesiastical structures throughout her history. Today, there are hierarchical institutions like the Roman Catholic, Eastern Orthodox, or Anglican churches. Other traditions are more democratically structured, like synods and presbyterial churches. There are also Baptist churches that only loosely affiliate, nondenominational churches that have no larger affiliation, and even house churches or small gatherings of Christians without the larger trappings of an institution. Each of these structures evolved in a specific setting, responding to the pressures or opportunities of their political and cultural moment. We don't have space here to explore the movements that led to the various forms of church governance we have today. However, church institutions tend to mimic their surrounding political institutions, likely because that is what church members and leaders know, understand, and are predisposed to ideologically based on their cultural setting.

In our American twenty-first-century context, churches are often run like businesses, complete with business managers, strategic planning committees, organizational efficiency values, leadership seminars, and marketing strategies. As the Reformers said, church structure is adiaphora, but this set of institutional values has its dangers just like any other. In Kurt Marquart's dogmatic work on church governance, he suggests that American churches have come to think of themselves as business corporations that carry out Jesus' mission.[31] Our cultural assumption of what makes a successful business involves growth, financial stability, popularity, and significant reach and engagement. In the Church, this may translate to large, financially successful organizations with many members and highly attended outreach events.

However, when we use business strategies to further the Church's mission, we may unwittingly elevate organizational stability and efficiency over the truth and faithful proclamation of God's Word. We end up substituting the marks of effectiveness that the business world uses for those of Christ. I have witnessed this thinking in many churches today, often with well-meaning intentions. After all, who wants the Church to be ineffective? We love Jesus, and we want to do our best to help Jesus do His work. But when we elevate what works over what is most true, we act under the false assumption that efficiency and effectiveness are the most important considerations.

In the time of the Reformation, church tradition was exalted over the Word of God, and it led to the content of the faith being devalued and neglected. Today, we often emphasize effectiveness and institutional success based on business model assumptions over the Word of God, which also leads to the content of the faith being

---

31   Kurt Marquart, ed., *The Church and Her Fellowship, Ministry, and Governance*, Confessional Lutheran Dogmatics, vol. 9 (Northville, SD: The Luther Academy, 1990), 214.

devalued. This happens when we ask, "Is this church successful in reaching its goals?" or "Is this church working for me?" instead of, "Does this church teach the truth about Jesus Christ?"

When the emphasis shifts away from faith in Jesus Christ, His objective atonement, and the forgiveness of sins offered in the Sacraments to the individual member's experience of church, the church begins to treat the children of God as customers. If the church that draws in the most customers is the most effective, then the message of God's Law and Gospel can easily be replaced with a message that people like more: a message that centers on the individual's experiences, needs, desires, and emotions instead of on the work of Christ. Over time, this mentality can greatly harm our faith, both corporately and as individuals. This type of church structure may seem to offer comfort in the short term, but spiritual comfort is not the same as feeling comfortable. For example, a person may be comfortable with the notion that they do many good deeds and are therefore probably in good standing before God. That doesn't mean they have genuine assurance or comfort in their standing before God. Such comfort comes only from resting in the knowledge of what Christ has done for us on the cross.

Thinking of the church as a business also affects how we view the role of the pastor. In larger churches, we might think of pastors as CEOs or organizational leaders, tasked with setting a unique vision and goals for the congregation and ensuring the organization meets those goals. In smaller churches, we might think of the pastor as an employee, the person getting paid to "put church on" for the rest of us. Both of these ways of seeing the pastoral office miss the point—the pastor is there to preach and teach the Word of God.

Business-style marketing and strategizing within the church can also feed into the increasing sense of competition and tension between different churches. Certainly this tension exists between denominations, but if we are honest, it also exists within a single church body, even among churches that share a confession within the same synod, district, or city. When we employ marketing tactics and seek to "sell" people on the Christian faith, it encourages a consumer mentality about church.

Such marketing strategies, even if well-intentioned, demonstrate a lack of faith. If the Church is instituted by Jesus and sustained by the work of the Holy Spirit, we should not seek to sell its contents. Truth speaks for itself. When we create worship services, event opportunities, and resources solely based on what people *want*, we fail in the mission of the Church, which is to deliver what people *need*. Church no longer shapes us; we shape the church. And when the church is shaped not by God's truth but by our whims, the church is no longer a source of objective comfort and assurance. A church run by human desires—whether those of a powerful few or a catered-to many—has nothing objective and true to ground it.

The Gift of Authority

The structure of our churches should reflect God's values rather than our human values. While Scripture does not dictate precise governing structures for our churches, the New Testament is explicit about the authority given to the universal Church through the pastoral office. This office exists to preserve the Word of God from false teaching and to proclaim it faithfully to God's people. We all desperately need forgiveness of sins and a right relationship with our heavenly Father. The pastor images Christ to His Bride in the Divine Service by offering this forgiveness through the Word, the absolution of sins, and the Sacraments.

As sinners, we do not always know what we need. Sometimes we want our pastors or our churches to provide specific service times, amenities, or events for us. Sometimes we want to be emotionally stirred by vibrant musicians or to be told that our sins aren't a big deal or to be affirmed in our self-righteousness by hearing how other churches are doing it wrong. But what we need from our pastors and church leaders is to hear the truth of God's Word, unfiltered by our preferences and sinful desires. We need our pastor to reflect Jesus to us.

Jesus Himself encountered people who did not accept His Word. Scripture tells us that when our Lord preached, some turned away and did not believe Him. If this was true for Jesus, we should expect it to be true in our churches and for our pastors as well. Our pastors are called to be faithful to God's Word. They are not called to attract people to our church building, to increase giving, or to ensure that the various groups that meet in the church are adequately staffed or funded. Those things are tangential at best and distracting at worst. We should expect our pastors to focus on the gift that Jesus calls them to give to us—forgiveness through the Word and Sacraments.

> "When many of His disciples heard it, they said, 'This is a hard saying; who can listen to it?' But Jesus, knowing in Himself that His disciples were grumbling about this, said to them, 'Do you take offense at this? . . . The words that I have spoken to you are spirit and life. But there are some of you who do not believe.' . . . After this many of His disciples turned back and no longer walked with Him." (John 6:60–61, 63–64, 66).

On a practical level, this distinction between the scriptural Office of Public Ministry and the day-to-day realities of leading a church creates a tension that all pastors and churches wrestle with and settle in different ways. Our congregations today are like businesses in that they employ people, handle budgets, own and maintain facilities, and communicate with parishioners regularly. None of these things are wrong; Scripture does teach that pastors are to earn their living from the church (see 1 Corinthians 9:14), and we read in Acts that as the Church grew, new support positions were created to assist the apostles in overseeing tasks such as feeding the hungry (see Acts 6:2–4). This was done specifically so that the apostles could devote themselves to the teaching of the Word and to prayer.

It is appropriate for churches to call other members to serve in various ways, and the fact that a church is large and has an intricate staff and budget model is not wrong in and of itself. However, we never want to devalue the teaching of the Word and the administration of the Sacraments. All activities of a congregation should be seen as an extension of the preaching and teaching office. Therefore, the pastor should be respected and consulted in all things, and insofar as he holds God's Word before the people and rightly teaches it and administers the Sacraments, he should be honored, loved, and cared for by his congregation.

Final Thought

In the Garden of Eden, Adam was given the job of speaking God's Word to creation and leading those under his authority to depend on God and obey God's Word. When Adam failed in this calling, God sent His Son to do what man could not. Jesus is the perfect Head, the Word made flesh who dwelt among us and who still meets with us in His Word and Sacraments. The role of pastor is a gift Jesus has given to His Church to image His headship to His Bride, to safeguard and preach the Word, and to declare the forgiveness of sins to each of us. While the office of pastor is filled by sinful men who fail at times in their calling, it is still a good office, and the Holy

> This chapter on the pastoral office does not cover the controversy over women's ordination. To explore that topic, see chapter 7 of *Male and Female: Embracing Your Role in God's Design*, which I coauthored with my husband, Jonathan.

Spirit uses this office for our comfort and assurance. Your pastor is the person you can always go to in repentance with any sin, no matter how big, and your pastor must and should declare to you the full forgiveness that is yours because of Christ. This role is a gift for our comfort as we go through the trials and challenges of life in this sinful world. Jesus gives the Church pastors to teach the Word faithfully.

Discussion Questions

. . . .

1. Read Titus 1:5–9, a passage similar to 1 Timothy 3. What does this text teach us about the role of pastor?

2. What are some ways that we can honor the office of pastor and support our pastors in our churches? What do you think are some of the challenges pastors and their families face in ministry?

3. Compare and contrast the roles of parent/child with those of pastor/parishioner. How are these relationships similar? How are they different?

4. In what ways can the role of pastoral authority be abused or misused in the Church? Why is this especially harmful when it happens?

5. Share about a time when a pastor was a blessing in your life by bringing the Word of God into a situation where it was needed.

Lord of the Church, thank You for the gift of good authority. Thank You for all those in authority who fulfill their offices to Your glory. We especially praise You for godly parents, pastors, and government officials. We pray that You would guide and indwell those in positions of authority, that they may image Your justice, honor, love, and compassion to those under them. We pray that we would submit to those in authority over us out of reverence for You, placing our trust in You and upholding our leaders in prayer. We thank You especially for the gift of Your authoritative Word, the Bible, and for reserving final authority in both the Church and the world to Yourself. Forgive us when we seek to claim this authority for ourselves or for when we fail to trust in Your head ship in the Church. In Your name we pray. Amen.

Forgiveness and
the Sacraments

· ·

MARTIN CHEMNITZ

Martin Chemnitz (1522–86) was a second-generation German Lutheran reformer. He wrote, among other things, the Solid Declaration of the Formula of Concord and the four-volume *Examination of the Council of Trent*, which may be the most complete defense of the Christian faith against the errors of the Roman Catholic Church. He writes systematically, outlining a theological position, examining it first in light of Scripture and then in light of the Church Fathers, and finally applying these insights to the errors he is addressing. His knowledge of the Church Fathers is comprehensive, and while much of his writing is polemical (intended to speak against the errors of his contemporaries), his tone is measured and gracious whenever possible. I enjoy both his wit and his charitableness as he summarizes the teachings of Scripture and the historic Church.

In sixteenth-century Germany, the ruler of a region was responsible for the religious practices of that territory. After the Reformation, this meant that a territory was either Lutheran or Roman Catholic based on the current leader's convictions. When Duke Julius's father died, Julius tasked Chemnitz with converting the duchy from Catholicism to Lutheranism. As was common practice, Chemnitz wrote a "church order" to accomplish this—an outline of both the theology to be taught in the local churches and the liturgy and practices that should accompany and express this theology. In the following excerpt, he speaks to the comfort and certainty that proper observance of the Lord's Supper and Baptism grants to the faithful.

Because we thus in the Lord's Supper have great, glorious, rich, heavenly treasures and benefits, this Supper shall be held and used in the Christian churches with the highest reverence and in the same way as, and in no other way than, the Son of God ordained and commanded in His testament. . . .

Because, moreover, the Lord's Supper with its correct, true use from God's Word has now been entirely restored to these churches, the people are to be diligently exhorted to thank God heartily for it, and so in true thankfulness to make frequent use of the Supper, as Paul teaches, not out of compulsion, at designated times, but as their own need may drive them to it and as the great benefit, blessed comfort, and noble power of the Supper rouse them to it. This can be presented to them most simply from and with the Words of Institution, so that they may constantly have this exhortation before their eyes: "In true faith, let us be ever mindful of what Christ has bestowed upon us and never forget His death." Alas, we find that

we all too easily forget it and that the remembrance of it is weak, cold, and idle in us. But our dear Savior, Christ, calls out in His Supper: "Take, eat, drink. This is My body, My blood. Do this in remembrance of Me." Likewise, in holy Baptism we are included through Christ in the covenant of grace of the new testament. Alas, we do not keep this covenant as strictly and firmly as we ought. We often forsake and break this covenant. So in order that we may be certain that Christ again accepts us into this covenant of the new testament when we turn to Him in true repentance through faith, and so that we may have a certain pledge and seal that we may forever be found and remain in this covenant and be kept therein, the Son of God says in the Supper: "Drink of it, all of you. This cup is the new testament," etc. Likewise, the body of Christ is given for all, and His blood is shed for all. However, if you would like to be certain and sure whether God, by saying so, also means you personally, whether you also may be a partaker, and whether, in the face of God's judgment, you will be able to enjoy your blessedness and to take comfort in what Christ has earned and obtained with the offering of His body and with the shedding of His blood, then Christ not only promises these things to you in the general promise of the Gospel, or only through the mere word of the individual Absolution, but *He even confirms, seals, and certifies it for you with the highest pledge of all, namely, the very body which was given for you and the very blood which was shed for you. There, in the Supper, it is not a mere man who deals with you individually, but Christ, your Savior Himself, through His minister.*

And He says: "Take, eat. This is My body, which is given for you. Take, drink. This is My blood which is shed for you for the forgiveness of your sins," etc. Nothing good dwells in our flesh. The sin, which works many evil desires in us, hinders the good and often causes us to fall. Christ, however, in His Supper, engages with us in a blessed exchange whereby He unites Himself with us through His holy flesh and blood so that, by His power, He may continually crucify and kill the old Adam more and more. *And thus we all become one body in Christ, where each member is to love, honor, and support the other.* And, in summary, he who finds that he is weak in faith has in the Lord's Supper a blessed, powerful antidote to strengthen faith, etc. If this basis is diligently stressed, faithful Christians will find themselves partaking of the Lord's Supper often and with great devotion. And on this basis they can also be instructed regarding the benefit, fruit, and consolation which poor, troubled consciences find in the right use of the Lord's Supper. However, if a person will not permit himself to be moved by these reasons, it may be seen what sort of a Christian he is. But here a reminder must be given against the teaching of the work being efficacious by the outward action [*opus operatum*], so that the people do not think that they receive such great treasures and benefits for the sake of this work of theirs, when they go to the Lord's Supper. Rather, they are to be diligently admonished to examine themselves first so that they do not eat to their judgment in the Supper and become guilty of the body and blood of the Lord (1 Corinthians 11:[27–32]). And this examination consists in asking whether the person has a truly repentant heart that acknowledges its sins and is moved to sorrow over them. For where there is and remains a wicked intention to persist and continue in sin, there is a false examination. Above all, however, the true examination consists in the heart's seeking, requesting, grasping, and appropriating God's grace, forgiveness of sins, and salvation through true faith in the obedience, suffering, and death of the Lord Christ. For he who is thus disposed receives the Sacrament worthily, not to his judgment, but to the strengthening of his faith. And consciences are to be instructed that they should not let themselves be frightened away from the Lord's Supper when they find that their repentance is insignificant and cold, their faith weak, though they wish that their repentance were more fervent and their faith stronger. They should know that they are to make use of the Lord's Supper to the very end that these things may be strengthened and increased in them through the Lord Christ.[32]

In this selection, Chemnitz first emphasizes the comfort and certainty that the Sacraments provide for us. He then speaks about receiving the Sacrament worthily. Each of us should examine ourselves before partaking, and those who receive the Supper with an intent to continue in sin do so to their harm. However, we should not be scared to come forward. Our desire for a stronger repentance or faith is itself a sign that we are receiving Jesus' body and blood worthily. The blood of Christ is for us, and lest we doubt the truth of this statement, Jesus offers it to us literally as well.

---

32   Martin Chemnitz and Jacob Andreae, *Church Order for Braunschweig-Wolfenbüttel*, trans. Jacob Corzine, Matthew C. Harrison, and Andrew Smith, *Chemnitz's Works*, vol. 9 (St. Louis: Concordia Publishing House, 2015), 61, 62–64, emphasis added.

The External Word

. . . .

Y ou cannot offer comfort to yourself. I have tried on many occasions to comfort myself, and you probably have too, but it doesn't really work. Sometimes my mind gets going, and I lie awake in bed with racing, anxious thoughts. Sometimes I find myself questioning if people like me, if they find me fun to be around, if they think I'm too high maintenance. Sometimes I question my worth. We don't all have the same struggles, but we all have feelings of inadequacy or doubt at times. When this happens, we try to quiet our worries and fears with reassuring self-talk, but in my experience, comfort never comes without something external. We need a loved one to offer words of affirmation or a caring gesture. We need a reminder of the truth—someone to speak God's promises to us so we can flee from the lies of Satan that swirl inside our heads. Comfort always comes from outside of ourselves.

Comfort from God does not originate within us. We may feel like God whispers His comfort to our hearts, but if God is doing this, He is doing so through the Holy Spirit and through our recollections of His Word. That is how God works. Even when we are able to counter our anxious thoughts with true thoughts, those true thoughts come from outside of us, perhaps from Scripture we memorized in our childhood or the truthful words of a hymn or our recollection of a sermon in which we heard the Gospel preached.

Our heavenly Father wants to comfort us, and He provides that comfort and assurance in tangible ways. When we long to be drawn closer to our Lord, we can turn to the Church, which is His Body on earth. Through His Body, Jesus has provided His Word and His Sacraments to nurture our faith and sustain us in our walk with Him. Some of us have been hurt in the Church or have not experienced churches as places of comfort and nurture. For these and other reasons, it can be tempting to look outside of the Church for ways to become closer to God, and indeed we may find God-given comfort through other parts of His creation. Still, God has given us the gifts of Word and Sacrament within the Church so that we may know Him and grow in our faith.

Sometimes people feel that they connect better with God out in nature or that they can just as easily foster their relationship with Jesus at home on their own. We do not always see the need for the Church, perhaps because we are individualistic people, and we think of our relationship with God as very personal. I'm reminded of a moment in the book *Anne of Green Gables* when Anne wonders out loud:

> **Why must people kneel down to pray? If I really wanted to pray I'll tell you what I'd do. I'd go out into a great big field all alone or into the deep, deep woods, and I'd look up into the sky—up—up—up—into that lovely blue sky that looks as if there was no end to its blueness. And then I'd just *feel* a prayer.**[33]

There's nothing wrong with praying to God in a field or any-where else. All of creation points us to our Creator! However, we miss something about God's

In Lutheran hymnals, the orders of services are labeled not "Worship Service" but "Divine Service." Calling our weekly gatherings "the Divine Service" rightly names what is happening. When we gather, God is the one doing things. He is serving us through His Word and His Sacraments. He offers us forgiveness, His Word, and strength and encouragement for our week and lives. Of course, we sing songs of thanksgiving and offer our prayers in response to God's goodness and love, but the primary actor in the service is God, not us.

---

33   L. M. Montgomery, *Anne of Green Gables* (New York: Skylark Books, 1908), 51.

nature with this vein of thinking. Anne thinks of God as something mystical, something impersonal, something that is more easily accessed through the natural world than through specific relational means. Our God is not distant, impersonal, or merely the Creator of our world. He is *personal*, and He has told us where we can go to meet Him!

Baptized into the Body

. . . . .

We enter the Church through the waters of Baptism. For many of us, Baptism is the initial instance of the external Word meeting us where we are, forgiving our sins, and giving the gift of the Holy Spirit and faith to grasp God's promises. In my living room, we have a piece of wall art featuring Romans 6:4–5:

> **We were buried therefore with Him by baptism into death, in order that, just as Christ was raised from the dead by the glory of the Father, we too might walk in newness of life. For if we have been united with Him in a death like His, we shall certainly be united with Him in a resurrection like His.**

I put these verses up in our home because of the objective certainty these words provide. We are all baptized into Jesus' death and resurrection. Baptism applies to each of us the atoning work of Jesus on the cross and His resurrection victory over death. The redemption story of God saving the world is now also the story of us. It's our story, not because of anything we've done but because of what Jesus has done.

At times, I have heard the critique that Lutherans place our faith in Baptism rather than in Jesus. We talk with such certainty about remembering our Baptism and cling to the promise that "Baptism . . . now saves you" (1 Peter 3:21), and this can sound to others like we are professing a kind of salvation by works, with Baptism being the work. We would say, however, that Baptism is a means by which Jesus promises to work salvation in our hearts through the faith He gives in Baptism. So yes, we do believe in salvation by works—works that God performs, not us. In Baptism, the pastor says the words and administers the water, but God is the *only* one doing the work of applying His promises to the person being baptized. This is why we baptize babies; while they may not understand what is going on, they don't have to. God is welcoming them into His family, and just as we welcome our children into our family without their consent or comprehension, God does the same for His.

Of course, Baptism is not the only way a person comes to faith. In adult converts, faith is given by the Holy Spirit before they receive Holy Baptism. Adults make a profession of faith before entering the family of God through the waters of Baptism because God's work in our hearts can be refused. It is possible to reject the Holy Spirit, so adults who receive Baptism profess the faith into which they will be baptized. Little children who receive Baptism are accompanied by parents and sponsors who solemnly promise to teach them this faith so that they may know the promises of God and understand the gift they have been given. But for all of us, our Baptism provides an external identity. We can take comfort in knowing that the most foundational truth about who we are is that we are God's children, and our Baptism is the literal, material place and moment in time in which we know that we entered into God's family. The certainty of this truth is an anchor we can cling to in all seasons and struggles of life.

> For more information on the Lutheran view of Baptism, see *Luther's Small Catechism with Explanation* on Baptism (pp. 285–305).

The Communion of Saints

. . . .

We enter the family of faith as individuals through Baptism, but we are made into one entity, one Body, one Church through our participation in the Lord's Supper, where Christ regularly meets with us. If Baptism is the individual Sacrament in which you are called by name and Christ's atoning work on the cross is applied to you specifically, then Communion is the corporate Sacrament in which we are bound both to Christ and to one another. We read this in Paul's Letter to the Corinthian Church: "The cup of blessing that we bless, is it not a participation in the blood of Christ? The bread that we break, is it not a participation in the body of Christ? Because there is one bread, we who are many are one body, for we all partake of the one bread" (1 Corinthians 10:16–17).

> For a more thorough exploration of the Lutheran view of Communion, see *Luther's Small Catechism with Explanation* on the Lord's Supper (pp. 322–45).

As Lutheran Christians, we believe in the real presence of Jesus in Holy Communion. We believe that when Jesus says, "This is My body," and "This is My blood," He means this literally; He is truly present in the bread and the wine. Many Christians do not hold to this teaching, believing rather that Jesus is speaking figuratively and that the bread and the wine are mere representations of His body and blood.

Consider, however, that Jesus' words are not like our words. In John's Gospel, we read, "In the beginning was the Word, and the Word was with God, and the Word was God. He was in the beginning with God. All things were made through Him, and without Him was not any thing made that was made" (1:1–3). Jesus is the Word that spoke all things into existence. He is the one who said, "'Let there be light,' and there was light" (Genesis 1:3). When the

Word of God speaks, what He says comes into existence. When Jesus speaks, He does not merely describe what He sees (as we do when we speak) but actually creates reality. If Jesus says, "Your sins are forgiven," we have faith in His Word that it is so. When Jesus says, "This is My body," we likewise have faith in His Word. In John 1:14, we read that "the Word became flesh and dwelt among us." If God can become a man and dwell among us, He can also be bodily present in bread and wine.

We may not understand how this is true or be able to fully wrap our minds around it, but that doesn't make it any less true. There are many things that a young child cannot understand, but that doesn't make those things untrue. The truth and the mystery of what Jesus does for us in the Sacraments should be approached similarly. We may hold onto a belief sincerely even as we do not comprehend it entirely.

Just as there is only one Christ, so also there is only one Church. This one, universal Church spread throughout the world is made up of many local congregations that faithfully gather around Christ's Word and Sacraments. Jesus sees this universal Church as His Bride. We draw comfort from belonging to this Body, and we profess faith in God's work in and through us as this Church. Our fellow Christians will therefore care for one another in ways that image Christ's love. However, sometimes our sin gets the better of us, and a church or its members will fail to uphold the truth of God's love in either their teachings or practices. In these cases, we experience church as hurtful. While sometimes a local church may fail us, the Bride of Christ still exists. We can continue to draw comfort from belonging

> "There is one body and one Spirit—just as you were called to the one hope that belongs to your call—one Lord, one faith, one baptism, one God and Father of all, who is over all and through all and in all."
> (Ephesians 4:4–6)

to the Body, even when a specific part of that Body does not reflect the loving servant-leadership of the Head.

Closed Communion

There has never been a period of theological purity in the history of the Church. The Holy Spirit always works through the Word to preserve the faith, but from Paul's New Testament letters until today, there has always been discord, tension, and struggle over matters of doctrine. Honestly, this should not surprise us. Jesus says that He is the truth, which means that the very identity of our God is on the line when we talk about doctrinal disagreements. We are not omniscient like God, but God does reveal His plan of salvation to us in His Word. This is why we can hope to understand the Bible and the things of God, even while knowing that not everyone will accept these truths in their purity.

In the reception of Holy Communion, tension over doctrinal differences is often highlighted. In a larger discussion about Communion and division, Paul says that "as often as you eat this bread and drink the cup, you proclaim the Lord's death until He comes" (1 Corinthians 11:26). Here, he shows that communing together is connected to our proclamation of Christ—our profession of faith. This leads us to the topic of closed Communion, which is the practice of communing only those who share the same confession of faith.

Historically, Communion has always been linked to church fellowship and doctrinal unity. For example, in the first few centuries of the Church, adult converts would often spend three years in catechesis to prepare for reception into the congregation. During this time, the catechumens would attend worship faithfully to listen and learn, but they would not commune. At the end of the process, they would make a public profession of faith, sometimes accompanied by a series of questions to make sure they truly understood their profession, before being baptized and admitted to the altar.

As we saw in chapter 4, doctrinal disagreements have always mattered in the Church, and closed Communion is an expression of that. The practice is not new. Admitting or not admitting fellow Christians to the Lord's Supper was universally understood as communicating that the profession of faith was either shared in its entirety or differed significantly. In practicing judicious admission to the Lord's Table, pastors were seen as the defenders against heresy according to their office as the public teacher of the Word.

Jesus says, "I am the way, and the truth, and the life" (John 14:6). This is not figurative. As the Word, He is literally the embodied Truth that holds all things together. Jesus also says that we are united with Him and with one another in His Supper. If we commune with people who do not confess the Truth as we do, we are being united with untruth. This is blasphemous and is a misuse of the Sacrament.[34] We participate in Christ's body together in a real sense in the Sacrament. In church bodies where Communion is understood only as a representation or symbol, there is less felt necessity for closed Communion and therefore a lessened emphasis. But we know the power of the Lord's Supper and its significance, and we humbly submit to the scriptural admonitions to "discern the body" (see 1 Corinthians 11:29) and to "be reconciled" to one another (see Matthew 5:23–24).

When we participate in the Sacrament, we receive Christ and are united with one another. We are professing unity of doctrine, which means that we are also professing unity of practice. In chapter 3, we explored how the Holy Spirit sanctifies us through the Church—that our practice flows out of our doctrine. When we practice something against God's Word in a willful and unrepentant

---

34 In 1 Corinthians 10, Paul links his instructions regarding Communion to a discussion of idolatry. By participating with those who hold different beliefs, we unite ourselves to those beliefs—hence the blasphemy.

way, we are professing that practice with our actions. This is why pastors will at times refuse to commune church members living in unrepentant sin. It is the same principle as not communing those who profess a different belief with their words: those living in open sin profess a differing belief with their actions.

This may feel challenging, but we are called to live in the truth. John's epistle teaches this concept much better than I can:

> This is the message we have heard from Him and proclaim to you, that God is light, and in Him is no darkness at all. If we say we have fellowship with Him while we walk in darkness, we lie and do not practice the truth. But if we walk in the light, as He is in the light, we have fellowship with one another, and the blood of Jesus His Son cleanses us from all sin. If we say we have no sin, we deceive ourselves, and the truth is not in us. If we confess our sins, He is faithful and just to forgive us our sins and to cleanse us from all unrighteousness. If we say we have not sinned, we make Him a liar, and His word is not in us. (1 John 1:5–10)

In my experience, closed Communion is a sensitive topic. I have had many conversations with compassionate, caring Christians who struggle to accept their church's practice. It can seem mean or judgmental to refuse Communion to someone because he or she believes differently than we do. I think this is partly a result of our overly individualistic society and our comfort with relativism. We're not used to thinking corporately. Most of us intuitively think about our spiritual lives as individual pursuits, and our culture tells us not to challenge other people's "spiritual journeys." We don't want to presume to tell people what they do or do not understand about something as personal as religion.

I understand the discomfort of telling people that they are incorrect about something or of pointing out significant areas of disagreement. But I think the real reason we're uncomfortable with closed Communion is because it forces us to be honest about division, and division is painful. Many of us have family members who are Christians but who belong to different church bodies. We grieve that we cannot come to the Lord's Table together. I often hear people say something like, "I want to commune with my children and my grandchildren when I visit them or when they visit me. It doesn't seem right that I cannot do that." And that's true: it isn't right. In a perfect world—in the perfect world that is to come—our divisions will cease. But for now, we profess faith in that final marriage feast to come by keeping the Supper sacred and being honest about the state of our relationships with God and with one another.

Sometimes people advocate for the practice of open Communion by pointing out this unity that believers will have on the final day, at the marriage feast of the Lamb. They suggest that our practice of Communion now should reflect our eschatological hope that we will all be made one in Christ when He returns. Open Communion, therefore, is a profession of faith in the unity we will have in the new creation to come. But this fails to deal honestly with the division that exists today. As discussed in chapter 4, we become united as one Body not by feigning unity with one another now but by uniting ourselves to Christ. In Him, and only in Him, are we made into that Body.

In John 4:24, Jesus tells the woman at the well that "God is spirit, and those who worship Him must worship in spirit and in truth." Recognizing that our unity in the Sacrament is both spiritual and grounded in God's truth, we hold one another to that standard of truth when we partake of Christ's body and blood. We love one another best as members of the Body when we are honest, humble, and sincere in our confession of faith and our admonitions to one another. We support one another best as fellow Christians when we hold fast to Jesus, who is the truth, even when that truth makes us uncomfortable by showing us the sin and disunity that surround us. Genuine comfort is not the absence of conflict but the peace that comes from standing in the truth.

Lex Orandi, Lex Credendi

*T*he Latin phrase *lex orandi, lex credendi* literally translates to "the law of what is prayed is the law of what is believed." In other words, how we pray or worship is (or becomes) what we believe. Our practices in our local congregations matter a great deal because they form our thinking and our beliefs. Over time, bad practices will create false beliefs in us, resulting in spiritual struggles when life presents us with challenges. Consider these examples:

- **If you baptize only adults, you come to believe that Baptism has something to do with mature understanding or the ability to make decisions.**

- **If you sing songs only focused on our emotional response to God, you come to believe you need to have an emotional response to have a valid spiritual experience.**

- **If you commune with everyone, even those who hold vastly different understandings of what it means to believe in Jesus, you come to believe that the details of the faith do not matter.**

- **If you only practice extemporaneous prayer, you come to believe that only your heart and feelings in the moment can guide you spiritually.**

- **If you never pray extemporaneously, you come to believe that you can't talk to God about your life or that God doesn't care about you personally.**

- **If you shun all things old or traditional in favor of experiences that feel more authentic, you come to believe that those faithful who came before us did not have relevant, authentic faith, and therefore there is no wisdom to be gained from their writings and experiences.**

This book is about the gift of comfort that Jesus gives us through the Church, and that comfort comes in the objective, rooted, unchanging nature of the Church. The Church is comforting because Jesus, the Head of the Church, offers us comfort and security within her. Our practices when we gather in worship should reflect this and point to the truth we profess. That truth is Jesus for us. This is what the Divine Service is all about.

Final Thought

When Jesus was incarnate and born as a man, the God of the universe walked, talked, and ate with us. And now that Jesus has ascended, He still meets with us personally, tactilely, and specifically in His Sacraments. If you wanted to meet with a friend and get to know them better, and they had told you exactly where they would be and at what time, would you go to that place and meet them? Or would you go to a place that you enjoy and hope to mystically feel their presence somehow? That's an easy answer! We must meet with our Lord where He promises to be: in the fellowship of the faithful, gathered by Christ around His Word and His Sacraments. As He says, "Where two or three are gathered in My name, there I am among them" (Matthew 18:20). Jesus gives the Church Himself in the Sacraments to strengthen the Body of Christ.

Discussion Questions

· · · · · · · · · · · · · · · · · · · ·

1. Look back over the excerpt from Martin Chemnitz's *Church Order* at the beginning of the chapter. Highlight any parts you find particularly comforting. How does Chemnitz encourage us to draw comfort from the Lord's Supper? What does the Lord's Supper do for our faith?

2. Read 1 Corinthians 10:1–22. What does this passage teach us about Communion? What does it teach us about what it means to be the Body of Christ?

3. Consider the phrase *lex orandi, lex credendi.* Can you think of examples from your life of practices that have subtly affected your beliefs, perhaps without you noticing?

4. This chapter covered some specific beliefs regarding Baptism and Communion. What did you learn or realize about the Sacraments? Do you have any questions about these topics? Write them down and ask your pastor!

Heavenly Father, thank You for interacting with us in tangible ways that involve all of our senses and that reaffirm the value You place on this physical world. Thank You for the gifts of Baptism and Holy Communion. Forgive us for the times when we have not been appreciative of the Sacraments and have devalued them or failed to understand them as You have revealed them in Your Word. Help us to live every day in repentance and faith in Your forgiveness. Embolden us to share the Good News of that forgiveness with others. In Jesus' name we pray. Amen.

Hope and the Growth of the Church

···

JOHN CHRYSOSTOM

John Chrysostom lived from AD 347 to 407 and served as bishop of Constantinople (in modern-day Turkey). The name *Chrysostom*, meaning "the golden-mouthed," was given to him after his death in recognition of his oratorical skill. Initially a lawyer, he became a Christian in his early twenties and adopted a monastic lifestyle. He was consecrated as bishop in 398, after which he worked to reform the Church and challenged the wealthy and politically powerful to lead a more generous, decent life in light of their faith and responsibilities to their fellow brothers and sisters in the Church. His life ended in exile, but shortly after his death, his legacy was restored, and he is viewed with honor in both the Western and Eastern Church traditions.

In this section from his sermon on Matthew 28, Chrysostom expounds upon the well-known passage often referred to as the Great Commission. He links this text both to comfort and to our eschatological hope in the life to come.

What does [Jesus] finally say to [the disciples] when he sees them? "All authority in heaven and on earth has been given to me." He is still speaking to them according to his humanity, for they had not yet received the Spirit which was able to raise them to higher things. "Go therefore and make disciples of all nations, baptizing them in the name of the Father and of the Son and of the Holy Spirit, teaching them to observe all that I have commanded you; and lo, I am with you always, to the close of the age." He gives them one charge with a view toward teaching and another charge concerning his commandments. He makes no mention of the future of the Jews. He does not scold Peter for his denial or any one of the others for their flight. Having put into their hands a summary of Christian teaching, which is expressed in the form of baptism, he commands them to go out into the whole world. . . .

After that, because he had enjoined on them great things, to raise their courage he reassures them that he will be with them always, "even to the end of the world." Now do you see the relation of his glory to his previous condescension? His own proper power is again restored. What he had said previously was spoken during the time of his humiliation.

He promised to be not only with these disciples but also with all who would subsequently believe after them. Jesus speaks to all believers as if to one body.

Do not speak to me, he says, of the difficulties you will
face, for "I am with you," as the one who makes all
things easy. Remember that this is also said repeatedly
to the prophets in the Old Testament. Recall Jeremiah
objecting that he is too young and Moses and Ezekiel
shrinking from the prophet's office. "I am with you"
is spoken to all these people. . . .

Observe the excellence of those who were sent out
into the whole world. Others who were called found
ways of excusing themselves. But these did not beg off.

Jesus reminds his disciples of the consummation of
all things. He seeks to draw them further on, that they
may not look at the present dangers only but also at
the good things to come that last forever. He is in effect
saying, "These difficult things that you will undergo
are soon to be finished with this present life. For this
world will come to an end. But the good things you are
to enjoy are immortal, as I have often told you before."
Having invigorated and roused their minds by the
remembrance of that coming day, he sent them out.[35]

In this homily, Chrysostom highlights that after the command to go out into the whole world and make disciples, Jesus promises that His comfort and His presence will always be with His Body. We do not go out alone, and the reason that we are to go out into the world is because we have hope—Jesus will not be gone forever. He is coming back!

---

35 John Chrysostom, "The Gospel of Matthew, Homily 90.2," in *Matthew 14–28*, ed. Manlio Simonetti, Ancient Christian Commentary on Scripture, vol. 1b (Downers Grove, IL: InterVarsity Press, 2002), 313–14, used by permission.

The Great Commission

· ·

When I was in middle school, I took a calligraphy class. For one project, I wrote out and illustrated Matthew 28:18–20. I chose to write the word *GO* in larger letters, emphasizing it visually in my presentation of the verse. It seemed to me, looking at the verse in my Bible at the time, that the emphasis was behind that word—we are supposed to go! I was taught that this passage meant we need to get out there and share the Gospel quickly, before it's too late. I think that was the general attitude toward evangelism in the Christian circles I was in as a child. This led me to feel guilt and uncertainty at times because I wasn't sure whether I was sharing the Gospel enough.

But I was missing some important aspects of this passage. Look at the wider context of these verses:

> Now the eleven disciples went to Galilee, to the mountain to which Jesus had directed them. And when they saw Him they worshiped Him, but some doubted. And Jesus came and said to them, "All authority in heaven and on earth has been given to Me. Go therefore and make disciples of all nations, baptizing them in the name of the Father and of the Son and of the Holy Spirit, teaching them to observe all that I have commanded you. And behold, I am with you always, to the end of the age." (Matthew 28:16–20)

This text has been referred to as "the Great Commission" for only the past few hundred years of Church history. Today we associate it almost exclusively with evangelism, but commentaries from Early Church Fathers do not consider Jesus' command to make disciples as the primary message in these verses. Notice what comes right before Jesus' well-known words: "They worshiped Him, but some doubted" (v. 17). Jesus responds to their doubt with words of comfort. He reminds them that all authority in heaven and on earth is His. Jesus is in control. Because He is in control of all things here and all things to come, we can go forward confidently, making disciples by baptizing and teaching, and through all of this, Jesus promises to be with us to the end of the age. This is the last time Jesus speaks to His disciples before ascending into heaven. His final words are those of reassurance. As discussed in chapter 1, Jesus is the one who builds His Church. All things are under His authority.

Contrary to my assumption as a reader of the English translation, in the original Greek language, the verb in verse 18 is not "go." It is actually "make disciples." Another good translation might be "as you go along, make disciples." The emphasis is not on us stopping everything to run to the corners of the earth with the Gospel message (although some people are called to do this!). Instead, we are called to go through our lives in a way that makes disciples by baptizing people in the name of the triune God and teaching them to obey all that Jesus has commanded. More than a command, it is a promise of what will come. Growth will come through the teaching of Jesus' commandments as we go about our individual lives and callings. And not only will Jesus be with us in this age, but He will also come back.

Growth in the Early Church

*D*uring the first few centuries of Christianity, the Church grew rapidly. The faithful went from a group small enough to be locked in one room in Jerusalem on Pentecost morning to over three thousand people by that evening. Within a hundred years, it grew to a religion spanning the entire Roman Empire and beyond. By the time Emperor Constantine made Christianity legal in AD 313, there were millions of Christians throughout the world. The faith spread rapidly, even during hundreds of years of on-and-off persecution. It was often dangerous to be a Christian, yet the Church still grew by the power of the Holy Spirit.

Gathering together for worship presented a very real danger to the Early Church. Yet everywhere there were Christians, the faithful gathered at least weekly, if not more often. Evangelism of an illegal religion was also dangerous and challenging. Yet early Christians did both of these things—gathering and evangelizing—relentlessly, and the Church grew exponentially.

Conversion was a completely foreign concept to those with whom the first Christians would have interacted. Ancient religion was not generally exclusive; it was customary to add elements from any religious cult that one liked. This would have made Christianity both confusing and offensive, as Christians made an exclusive claim that *only Jesus* was to be worshiped as the one true God.[36] To convert to Christianity, they could not simply add the Christian beliefs and practices to their lives; they would also have to give up all ritual practices that worshiped false gods. This was the most challenging part for early converts.

If we are honest with ourselves, this is still the hardest part. People don't typically have a problem with Jesus loving them until belief in Jesus means they need to change their lifestyle, give up their idols, and live for Him instead of themselves. This reminds me of the rich young ruler in Matthew 19:16–22. In this passage, a young man approached Jesus, asking what he must do to be saved. Jesus told him to keep God's Law, and the young man responded that he had done so. Jesus then asked him to give up his wealth and follow Him, and the man went away sad.

---

36   Michael Green, *Evangelism in the Early Church* (Grand Rapids, MI: William B. Eerdmans Publishing Company, 2004), 206.

In his book *Evangelism in the Early Church*, Michael Green lists three components of evangelistic efforts in the first few centuries: first, a denial of any kind of universalism; second, a consciousness that Christians have a responsibility to reach the lost; and third, a coherent eschatology (or theology of the end times and our ultimate hope). Green asserts that some of our present-day struggles in evangelism are that people no longer believe in heaven or hell and that Christians cannot articulate a biblical eschatology as a concrete hope for the world.[37]

A few decades ago, it was common to begin evangelistic conversations by asking, "Do you know where you would go if you died today?" This question does not resonate with unbelievers today because belief in heaven and hell is no longer ingrained in our cultural consciousness. But this should not deter us from sharing the hope we have in Christ. Our hope is not merely in not going to hell. We have a much more comprehensive and beautiful eschatological hope than that!

We have a God who is putting an end to pain, suffering, evil, wrongdoing, sin, and all that is broken with our world. He is doing this through the cross and resurrection of Jesus, and it will be completed when Jesus returns again. The world still needs to hear this message.

Misconceptions about Evangelism

As a Christian in America in the twenty-first century, I am accustomed to seeing and hearing people panic over the future of the Church. Each decade brings our culture farther from an outwardly Christian set of social norms and into an increasingly hostile environment for the faithful. I empathize with my fellow Christians whose hearts hurt for the lost and those who simply fear

---

37 Green, *Evangelism in the Early Church*, 381–83.

for their society and the world that their children and grandchildren will inhabit. However, our response to these issues may not always reflect what the Bible teaches about the way the Gospel spreads and the Church grows.

The first misstep is that we can forget that Christ is the one who builds the Church. In chapter 1, we traced the promises that God made to His people from Genesis to Revelation. The promise made to Abraham, Isaac, and Jacob that all nations of the world would be blessed through them is ultimately fulfilled in Jesus' coming. In Isaiah, we read these prophetic words about the hope we have:

> On this mountain the LORD of hosts will make for all
> peoples a feast of rich food, a feast of well-aged wine,
> of rich food full of marrow, of aged wine well refined.
> And He will swallow up on this mountain the covering
> that is cast over all peoples, the veil that is spread over
> all nations. He will swallow up death forever; and the
> Lord GOD will wipe away tears from all faces, and the
> reproach of His people He will take away from all the
> earth, for the LORD has spoken. It will be said on that
> day, "Behold, this is our God; we have waited for Him,
> that He might save us. This is the LORD; we have waited
> for Him; let us be glad and rejoice in His salvation."
> (25:6–9)

Notice who is doing the saving in this passage: God is the one who gathers all nations to Himself. The Holy Spirit works through the Church to accomplish this, but who is the Head of the Church? Jesus. We do not grow the Church. Jesus does. This does not mean we should be apathetic or uncaring about those who do not know Him. But we do not need to feel anxious or overwhelmed by guilt and concern for something that Jesus has promised to accomplish. Jesus works to grow His Church in the specific ways that He has promised to work—through His Word and Sacraments. The words of a well-known hymn come to mind:

> **I am trusting Thee, Lord Jesus, Trusting only Thee;**
> **Trusting Thee for full salvation, Great and free. (*LSB***
> **729:1)**

If we trust our Lord Jesus for our own salvation, how much more must we place our trust in Him for the salvation of our neighbors.

The second error that hurts our ability to share the Gospel is the temptation to de-emphasize the content of the faith. In chapter 2, we learned that the Church is built around a specific creed—a rule of faith or statement of belief that is unchanging and objectively true. All three elements of Early Church evangelism noted above pertain to our knowledge of and ability to articulate the points of our faith. For example, we cannot refute universalism without knowing what Jesus taught and what He meant when He said, "I am the way, and the truth, and the life. No one comes to the Father except through Me" (John 14:6). We cannot read the exhortation to "in your hearts honor Christ the Lord as holy, always being prepared to make a defense to anyone who asks you for a reason for the hope that is in you; yet do it with gentleness and respect" (1 Peter 3:15) without seeing that God expects us to reach out with the truth to those who are lost. And perhaps most challenging, Christians cannot share a coherent eschatology with those who need to hear our hope if we do not know what we are hoping for and expecting in the second coming.

If you want to be better at sharing your faith with your family, friends, and co-workers, spend more time immersed in God's Word and studying doctrine. This will help you be prepared to speak into life's difficult situations. When we take the time to learn our faith in greater detail, we witness to the transformative power of the Word in our own lives and equip ourselves with words that the Holy Spirit can use to reach others through us.

Teaching God's Word is itself evangelistic because the Holy Spirit works through the Word. Parents who spend time in God's Word and learn the rich depth of our faith are better equipped to speak the truth to their children when challenging situations arise. When a friend brings up a topic related to faith, we will feel more prepared to share our faith when we know that faith well. If we are encouraged to wrestle with faith questions and seek answers from trusted pastors or theologians, we will be better able to stand firm in our faith when facing outside pressure or scrutiny. There is nothing wrong with not knowing the answer or responding with "I don't know, but that's a great question!" But we should nurture in one another a curiosity and longing to know the truth more and more each day.

Many New Testament verses call us to seek spiritual maturity and grow in our faith. Writing to the Colossians, Paul says, "And so, from the day we heard, we have not ceased to pray for you, asking that you may be filled with the knowledge of His will in all spiritual wisdom and understanding, so as to walk in a manner worthy of the Lord, fully pleasing to Him: bearing fruit in every good work and increasing in the knowledge of God" (1:9–10). The writer of Hebrews chastises the congregation for not growing in their knowledge of the Word:

> **For though by this time you ought to be teachers, you need someone to teach you again the basic principles of the oracles of God. You need milk, not solid food, for everyone who lives on milk is unskilled in the word of righteousness, since he is a child. But solid food is for the mature, for those who have their powers of discernment trained by constant practice to distinguish good from evil. (5:12–14)**

This admonishment is heavy: "Everyone who lives on milk is unskilled in the word of righteousness" (v. 13). The epistles clearly instruct the Church not to be satisfied with simplistic spiritual understanding. We are to desire to grow in our knowledge so that we may mature in our discernment, be better able to distinguish good from evil, and teach others God's Word as we go through life.

The third error that hurts our ability to share the Gospel is when we pit outreach against the life of the Church. This false dichotomy between outreach programs and instruction for church members stems from a

> For more verses on spiritual maturity, see 1 Peter 2:2–3; 1 Corinthians 1:1–3; and 1 Corinthians 14:20.

mistaken theological assumption that believers and unbelievers need to hear two different messages from the Church.

In much of American Christianity, there are evangelistic messages that proclaim the news of Jesus' death and resurrection for the remission of sins and end with an invitation to make a decision for Jesus or to accept Jesus into one's heart. Within such a framework, unbelievers need to hear this message, but those who already believe do not; they have already accepted Jesus. Instead, believers need to hear how to apply the Bible's teachings to their lives so they can live in a more holy, God-pleasing way. Because there are two different messages, events targeting believers and unbelievers will be different. Even in churches that do not teach this decision theology, we can end up separating church events, thinking that unbelievers will be scared away if something is "too churchy."

The truth is believers and unbelievers alike need the same things. We all need Jesus. We all need our sins forgiven, whether it's the first time we've heard forgiveness proclaimed or the thousandth. We all need our faith strengthened by God's Word. The Holy Spirit uses the Word both to ignite faith in the hearts of those who have not heard it before and to strengthen faith in those of us who already believe. God's Word is the same for all of us, and the Holy Spirit meets each of us where we are as He wills.

In an increasingly secularized society, and perhaps in any society, the act of gathering every Sunday witnesses to our faith. When our kids don't participate in a Sunday morning sporting event because that time is held sacred for church, when we ask to switch shifts so we can attend church on Sunday mornings, when we turn down a Sunday brunch invitation with friends—these are all moments when we are witnessing to our faith by our practice. We demonstrate that our faith takes priority and point our children, grandchildren, and all who know us to the One in whom we hope. Gathering together has always fueled evangelism in the Church. When we gather together around the Word and the Sacraments, the Holy Spirit works through these means as He has promised to strengthen our faith, better equipping us to share that faith with others. The Church has never attracted people to Jesus with anything other than Jesus.

Have you ever felt pressure or guilt over evangelism? Have you ever lived in fear that you aren't doing enough to save your friend, co-worker, or family member? Then hear the truth of Scripture: Jesus takes responsibility for both your salvation and the salvation of those you love. When we believe the lie that we are responsible for our own salvation, it is a natural progression to believe we are also responsible for the salvation of others. Neither is true, and in fact, both are idolatry because they put us in the place of God.

Listen to Jesus' words regarding the lost in this passage:

> And Jesus went throughout all the cities and villages, teaching in their synagogues and proclaiming the gospel of the kingdom and healing every disease and every affliction. When He saw the crowds, He had compassion for them, because they were harassed and helpless, like sheep without a shepherd. Then He said to His disciples, "The harvest is plentiful, but the

**laborers are few; therefore pray earnestly to the Lord
of the harvest to send out laborers into His harvest."
(Matthew 9:35–38)**

In this text, Jesus instructed His disciples to pray earnestly to
the Lord of the harvest and yet retained the responsibility for that
harvest. We are to be filled with our Lord's compassion for the lost,
but God alone is responsible for the harvest. We are laborers and
partners in prayer, and we trust the Lord of the harvest to love and
care for the lost through us (and even in spite of us).

How Evangelism Happens

*E*vangelism flows naturally from the Church's faithfulness to the
Word of God. When we immerse ourselves in God's Word and
orient our lives around His gifts, this points others to Him. This kind
of life stands in stark contrast to the values displayed by the world.
If we want people to know our God, we must live differently, reflect-
ing the unconditional, nontransactional love that Jesus has for us.

We point people to God's love through our vocations. Paul
describes marriage as a picture of Christ and the Church. Therefore,
our godly marriages will witness to the world the kind of sacrificial
love that Christ has for His Bride.
Our attitude toward children
points to our belief in our Creator
when we live as if we believe that
children are a blessing from God
to receive with thankfulness
and not an option, a choice, or
a lifestyle to opt into or out of
as we may desire. Our care for
aging parents (even for parents
that have wronged us or are hard

> A *vocation* is a calling or task
> that we have in the context of
> relationship—parents, spouses,
> children, employees, friends,
> neighbors, and the like. God
> works through each of us in these
> roles to provide and care for
> others. All vocations are holy and
> pleasing to God when done out of
> love for God and for one another.

to love) is done out of respect for God and out of selfless love toward them. Our generosity with our money and possessions points to our faith that there is more to life than today and our understanding that God has given us our blessings to better equip us to serve our neighbors.

God shows His love to the world through our actions, but He also shows it through the revelation of His Word. When we share God's Word with unbelievers, it will not always be accepted. Scripture tells us that the things of God are folly and nonsense without the Spirit to illuminate them:

> For the word of the cross is folly to those who are per-
> ishing, but to us who are being saved it is the power of
> God. . . . For since, in the wisdom of God, the world did
> not know God through wisdom, it pleased God through
> the folly of what we preach to save those who believe.
> For Jews demand signs and Greeks seek wisdom, but we
> preach Christ crucified, a stumbling block to Jews and
> folly to Gentiles, but to those who are called, both Jews
> and Greeks, Christ the power of God and the wisdom
> of God. For the foolishness of God is wiser than
> men, and the weakness of God is stronger than men.
> (1 Corinthians 1:18, 21–25)

We preach Christ crucified. Our hope is in Him. We need to be reminded of this truth every day so that we may be strengthened to live out our vocations with the selfless love that comes only from Him and that points the world to Him.

Final Thought

· · · · · · · · · · · ·

*T*he Holy Spirit grows the Church, and Jesus takes responsibility for all of it. As we become more like Christ, our hearts ache for those who do not yet know His forgiveness and love. Our hearts also ache for those who have been hurt by the Church rather than pointed to Christ. We cannot bear the burden of the Lord of the harvest ourselves, but we are privileged to be able to share our hope in Jesus confidently with those whom God has placed in our lives.

We do not need to worry or despair over the future of the Church. Jesus is Lord of the harvest, and He has all things under His control. All we do is live out the hope we have in Him and share that hope with the world through our words and actions. Jesus gives the Church a hope to share with the world.

Discussion Questions
. . . .

1. Read Revelation 21:1–8. How does this passage articulate our eschatological hope? How might we use this passage to offer comfort or to share Jesus with those who need to hear about Him?

2. Have you ever thought of your time spent studying theology and God's Word as evangelism? How does learning the content of the faith help you in your ability to share it with others?

3. Think of a time when you wanted to share your faith with someone but were hesitant or unsure. What words of comfort and truth can you remind yourself of regarding that situation? What words of comfort and truth do you wish you had shared with that person at the time?

4. Consider the vocations God has given you. How do you teach and make disciples in those vocations?

Holy Spirit, thank You for Your work in and through the Church! Thank You for promising to work through the Word to create faith in the hearts of hearers. Forgive us for the times when we have mistakenly looked to our own strength and competencies to build the Church and reach the lost. Forgive us also for the times when we have become discouraged and been tempted to despair of Your work in the world. Remind us daily, through Your Word, that all things are under Jesus' sovereign reign, and work Your fruit of peace and patience in our hearts as we faithfully share Your Gospel with those You have placed in our lives. Build our trust in You so that we may point others to the source of our confidence. In Jesus' name. Amen.

The Church for You

Dietrich Bonhoeffer lived from 1906 to 1945. He was a German Lutheran pastor who held fast to his confession of faith during the Nazi regime in his homeland. As part of Hitler's reforms, pastors in the state church were forced to change their teachings, placing Nazi ideology over and above Scripture. Bonhoeffer was a founding member of the Confessing Church in Germany in opposition to this heretical, Nazi-controlled state church, operating an underground, illegal seminary to educate faithful pastors during that time. He was executed in 1945 under the charge of conspiring to assassinate Hitler. It was a tragic time in world history and a challenging one for the Church.

On Sunday, July 23, 1933, in Berlin, Bonhoeffer preached on Matthew 16—the passage in which Christ establishes the Church upon the rock of Peter's confession (discussed in chapter 5). To those of us who find ourselves living in a world where the Church appears to be crumbling, he offers the following encouragement:

Yet it is not we who are to build, but God. No human being builds the church, but Christ alone. Anyone who proposes to build the church is certainly already on the way to destroying it, because it will turn out to be a temple of idolatry, though the builder does not intend that or know it. We are to confess, while God builds. We are to preach, while God builds. We are to pray to God, while God builds. We do not know God's plan. We cannot see whether God is building up or taking down. It could be that the times that human beings judge to be times for knocking down structures would be, for God, times to do a lot of building, or that the great moments of the church from a human viewpoint are, for God, times for pulling it down. It is a great comfort that Christ gives to the church: "You confess, preach, bear witness to me, but I alone will do the building, wherever I am pleased to do so. Don't interfere with my orders. Church, if you do your own part right, then that is enough. But make sure you do it right. Don't look for anyone's opinion; don't ask them what they think. Don't keep calculating; don't look around for support from others. Not only must church remain church, but you, my church, confess, confess, confess" . . . Christ alone is your Lord; by his grace alone you live, just as you are. Christ is building.[38]

We live in challenging times, but we are not the first to do so. Generations of Christians have lived through war, persecution, doubt, threat of schism, and uncertainty about the future. Be comforted, as Bonhoeffer was, that we can trust Jesus with

38   Dietrich Bonhoeffer, "Sermon on Matthew 16:13–18," in *Berlin: 1932–1933*, ed. Carsten Nicolaisen, Ernst-Albert Scharffenorth, and Larry L. Rasmussen, trans. Isabel Best, David Higgins, and Douglas W. Stott, Dietrich Bonhoeffer Works, vol. 12 (Minneapolis: Augsburg Fortress, 2009), 469–70.

the future of His Church. We do not always need to see the big picture. We do not need to know what will happen in the next five, ten, or fifty years. We can simply confess the truth of the Gospel of Christ and trust Him to work all things for our good.

Now and Not Yet

. . . .

This whole book has been about seeing the Church through God's eyes. I pray you have been drawn into the vision of the Church given in Scripture, that the Church is made beautiful and seen as beautiful by her Savior. Hopefully you have seen how the Church is Jesus' gift to each of us through which He gives us His Word, faith, forgiveness, and the hope of His ultimate return and the complete restoration of our world.

While I pray that you find this vision of the Church encouraging, you have likely experienced the imperfections of the Church. As we await the second coming, we are still sinful and far from blameless in our conduct as God's people. We are declared righteous on account of Christ, and we hope for the life to come, but right now, God's people still fall short. The Church is beautiful and washed in Jesus' blood. The Church is also full of sinners and responsible for hurt and pain in the lives of many. This is the tension of the Christian life—the now and the not yet.

We must not minimize the reality that people are often hurt by the Church. Sometimes the institutions and relationships that should be the greatest blessing in our lives become those that hurt us the most. The Church is designed to point us to God and His love for us; this makes it a prime target for Satan's attacks. Whenever a person or institution holds spiritual authority, the risk of abuse within that relationship is magnified. Satan knows that pastors and church authority structures are there to image God to His people.

If Satan can attack one of these authority figures, he can do profound spiritual damage. When people are hurt by the abuse of spiritual authority, it creates an obstacle between them and God. They no longer see the Church or their pastor as a model of godly authority, and their perception of God is twisted to reflect their experiences of their abuser.

We know how damaging abuse is within marriage or parent-child relationships. Like the Church, these are special relationships instituted by God. Just as an abusive parent-child relationship or an abusive marriage can lead to feelings of confusion and guilt, so the misuse of church authority can lead to trauma and misplaced feelings of guilt for the victim. The Church is the Body of Christ in our world, the way that Jesus seeks to gather all people to Himself. When those claiming to represent the Church and God Himself use their spiritual authority to hurt others, this is grievous sin and causes incalculable damage. Jesus rebukes this kind of behavior in the strongest terms (see Matthew 23 for Jesus' reproach of the Pharisees). The Church abuses her authority when she turns the treasures she has been entrusted with against people. When creed, practice, or our ultimate hope are perverted, such teachings almost immediately become abusive.

Bad theology hurts people. Teaching a false creed causes people to place their trust in things other than Christ, which will lead to doubt, despair, and confusion and may lead to a rejection of the faith. There are as many examples of this as there are false teachings. Consider this teaching: You are a terrible sinner. You must truly be sorry for your sins and accept Jesus into your heart or you will go to hell. This articulation has led many young children to pray fearfully night after night, hoping that they were sorry enough for their sins and that they were sincere enough in their faith to earn heaven instead of the fires of hell.

Good theology takes this terrifying prospect and removes the fear. We teach our children that they are claimed by Jesus in their Baptism, that the faith they need to be saved is a gift from God that the Holy Spirit has already worked in their hearts, and that there is nothing they need to say or do to merit God's love and life with Him. What may appear as subtle theological nuance changes the teaching from "You better hope you're good enough and have a strong enough faith" to "Jesus loves you and has given you everything you need." This is the difference between trauma and security—the difference between abusive religion and the comfort of God's love.

The abuse and trauma of sinful practices within a congregation are even more obvious. Pastors or others in spiritual authority who commit sins of abuse or gross moral misconduct while claiming to represent Christ deeply scar their victims spiritually, physically, and emotionally. Church leaders image Christ to their fellow believers, thus their sins and failings hurt the whole Body. Therefore, the Church must take the practices of its representatives seriously. When sin is present in blatant, unrepentant ways in the Church, it must be called out and addressed. (See 1 Timothy 3:2–3.)

As stated in the Formula of Concord, "True, saving faith is not in people who lack contrition and sorrow and who have a wicked plan to remain and continue in sins."[39] We believe and teach the forgiveness of sins in Christ, but true repentance is necessary. The fruit of repentance is accepting the earthly consequences of one's actions. When pastors or other leaders are found guilty of sins like adultery or drunkenness, those who are repentant will accept with grace that they no longer meet the scriptural criteria for the position they formerly held. When we take our creed seriously in the Church, we are able to take our practice seriously as well. The right distinction of Law and Gospel allows us to declare sinners forgiven and also hold them to account.

---

39   Formula of Concord Solid Declaration III 26.

Sometimes errant theology is blatantly and traumatically harmful. In other cases, weak theological understanding may not cause obvious harm, but it deprives God's people of the comfort and assurance that should be theirs. This often occurs with a false eschatological hope.

One way our hope can be abused is through an unbiblical, weaponized theology of the end times. An obvious, although rare, example would be the various end-times cults that base their existence around a specific date of Jesus' return. Such groups convince people to give up their money and possessions and live in false expectation.

A subtle but more common example is when we neglect the biblical teaching of the new creation (a modern manifestation of the Gnostic heresy discussed in chapter 2). Often, Christians focus on the idea of going to heaven when we die, describing or imagining it as an eternal, disembodied worship service. Certainly we do go to heaven to be with Jesus when we die, but we also "look for the resurrection of the dead and the life of the world to come" (Nicene Creed). As a child, I worried that I would miss out on all the things I was excited to do in life if Jesus came back before I grew up. I knew conceptually that I would enjoy heaven, but it didn't sound as fun as growing up, getting married, having kids, and exploring the world. Then I would feel guilty because I knew I was supposed to prefer heaven to this earth. A full, biblical articulation of our hope in the world to come eliminates this worry and guilt by properly honoring how good this creation is and how beautiful our lives are intended to be. Our hopes, dreams, and the things that we love about life will carry over into the new creation in one way or another because Jesus' return means that He will be making all things new—not simply taking us away from here to a peaceful worship service.

In a related way, we can neglect to provide the comfort of our eschatological hope when we offer empty platitudes during times of suffering and loss. Phrases like "Jesus needed another angel in heaven" or "It's all a part of God's plan" are attempts to wash away pain and suffering with our own reason. When we gloss over the suffering these things cause, we fail to acknowledge that death, sickness, and pain are truly enemies of God. We confess and bear witness to our hope in Christ when we do not allow suffering and pain to keep us from being present with one another and bearing one another's burdens.

Abide in the Word

Having faith in Jesus means being honest about our dependence on our Savior. We acknowledge that, just as we cannot save ourselves and needed Him to go to the cross to take the punishment for sin, we also need and humbly accept the gifts He gives us in and through His Body, the Church. We trust that Jesus has given us the Church for our benefit and that we keep His commandment when we "do not despise preaching and His Word, but hold it sacred and gladly hear and learn it" (Small Catechism, Third Commandment).

> "Remember the Sabbath day by keeping it holy. *What does this mean?* We should fear and love God so that we do not despise preaching and His Word, but hold it sacred and gladly hear and learn it." (Small Catechism, Third Commandment)

Jesus teaches that we stay connected to Him through His Word. He says:

> **Already you are clean because of the word that I have spoken to you. Abide in Me, and I in you. As the branch cannot bear fruit by itself, unless it abides in the vine, neither can you, unless you abide in Me. I am the vine; you are the branches. Whoever abides in Me and I in him, he it is that bears much fruit, for apart from Me you can do nothing. (John 15:3–5)**

His Word makes us clean, and His Word dwelling in us produces fruit in our lives. The Christian life starts with and is sustained by the Word of God.

On a practical level, how do we live immersed in the Word of God? Naturally, reading our Bibles and studying them with other Christians (especially those who have been trained and gifted to teach the Word) should be essential in the life of all believers. I also encourage all Christians to fully embrace the gift of the pastoral office by going to your pastor with any and all of your theological questions, concerns, and struggles. Sometimes people may feel embarrassed or shy to speak to the pastor. Perhaps you do not want to appear ignorant. Perhaps you think your pastor will not have time for you or that your concerns aren't important enough to be worth his time. Or perhaps you have had negative experiences with authority figures in the church in the past.

Whatever the case may be, let me assure you that a good pastor will embrace your questions as you seek to understand God's Word and how it applies to your life. As a pastor's wife, I know that my husband loves the opportunities he has to meet with his parishioners one-on-one or in family settings to talk about faith and life together. He may be busy, but this is what he went into ministry to do: to be there for people and to teach the Word of God. Those things bring him joy in ministry. You can honor the vocations your pastors and other church workers have by approaching them when you believe they can help and allowing them to walk alongside you through life's ups and downs.

Pastors and other church workers are also good resources for Bible study recommendations or training in how to study God's Word. Because bad theology can lead to misplaced emphasis and even painful false beliefs, we should seek out resources that train us to discern good Bible study materials from the bad ones. This is why it is helpful to study some theology as well as to read your

Bible—so that when you hear the Bible falsely interpreted, you are able to identify the errors.

Practice the Faith

· · · · · · · · · · · · · · · ·

We often think of "practicing our faith" as all the things we need to *do*. We need to read our Bibles more, believe the right things, do the right things, be at church each week. Certainly, reading our Bible and putting our faith into practice is part of what it means to be Christian, but the Gospel beauty of the Church is that it isn't about what we do. It's about what Jesus has done for us. In the Church, we regularly receive forgiveness of sins and Communion with Christ and His Body. This is where we are fueled and equipped for our lives as Christians. We simply cannot do it on our own.

Receiving Jesus' gifts with humility and gratitude means prioritizing church attendance. When we reserve Sunday morning for church, we teach our minds, souls, and bodies to value the preaching of God's Word and the Sacraments. Sometimes things that seem unavoidable (like work schedules) can make church attendance difficult. However, we should do everything in our power to gather around the Word and Sacraments. Perhaps there are services at different times, or perhaps you could speak to your employer about your scheduling needs. Ultimately, our choices reflect our priorities. If you find that your other life choices are keeping you from the Lord's Table indefinitely, it is time to make significant changes.

When we keep the Sabbath holy, we not only obey God's Law and receive the gifts of forgiveness and strengthening of faith, but we also confess by our actions that our faith in God is the highest priority in our lives. This is worth the social discomfort or inconvenience of saying no to other opportunities for the sake of faithful church attendance!

Proclaim Our Hope!

. . . .

*F*inally, living out this faith also means being willing and able to tell others about the hope that is ours in Christ. As we learned in chapter 7, this does not necessarily mean proselytizing or going on mission trips. We live out our faith in the choices we make and the values our families embody. We live out our faith when we speak the truth of Jesus and His redeeming work into the struggles and life situations of those God has placed in our lives.

Sometimes having these conversations can seem daunting. One way we can build one another up in the Body of Christ in this task is by talking about our hope within our families and faith communities. The more you do something, the easier it gets. If you are not comfortable talking about your faith with co-workers or friends, start by talking about your faith with your parents, spouse, or children. Start small. Next time you are out for a walk with your kids and they comment on some aspect of nature, take that opportunity to mention the beauty of creation and that God not only created all things but still actively cares for and preserves them. Your kids may ask a follow-up question or share an insight of their own, and the next thing you know, you're talking about our trust in God to provide for all of our needs. The more we practice speaking about God, the easier it will be when we want to share our faith with someone who may not know Him.

In 1 Thessalonians 4:13, Paul encourages us not to grieve as those who have no hope. A beautiful way that we bear witness to our faith as Christians is in our approach to death, grief, and suffering. In these moments—staring into the face of our own mortality—we should look the most different from those in our world who have no hope. We know the rest of the story. We know that death has been defeated. We are able to endure pain, sickness, suffering, and death because we know that this life is not the end. We can come alongside others who are suffering and bear with them because we know that Jesus does this for us. Our hope is truly one of salvation, and when we live as people who believe this, others will be pointed to our Savior as well.

One of my favorite verses are these words of faith spoken by Job in the midst of incredible loss. Job had lost his family, his health, his possessions, all that he had. Yet these are his words: "For I know that my Redeemer lives, and at the last He will stand upon the earth. And after my skin has been thus destroyed, yet in my flesh I shall see God, whom I shall see for myself, and my eyes shall behold, and not another" (Job 19:25–27). This kind of hope is contagious.

This hope is received by us from the hands of those who have gone before. The Church is the means by which the faith is transmitted from generation to generation. Those of us who are parents are commanded in Scripture to teach our children this faith, but the task of passing on the Church's creed, practice, and hope to each generation is entrusted to all Christians. You are an important part of the Church, and God intends to use you to preserve and pass on the faith to those who do not know it today and also for generations to come. Whether you *like* the Church or not, if you are a believer and consider yourself a Christian, you are part of the Church. Each part of the Church is important, and the Body of Christ needs all of its members to work together, to build one another up, to teach, encourage, and serve one another in love, and to await Christ's return together as one, as the Book of Ephesians beautifully describes:

> And He gave the apostles, the prophets, the evangelists, the shepherds and teachers, to equip the saints for the work of ministry, for building up the body of Christ, until we all attain to the unity of the faith and of the knowledge of the Son of God, to mature manhood, to the measure of the stature of the fullness of Christ, so

that we may no longer be children, tossed to and fro by
the waves and carried about by every wind of doctrine,
by human cunning, by craftiness in deceitful schemes.
Rather, speaking the truth in love, we are to grow up
in every way into Him who is the Head, into Christ,
from whom the whole body, joined and held together by
every joint with which it is equipped, when each part is
working properly, makes the body grow so that it builds
itself up in love. (Ephesians 4:11–16)

Final Thought

· · · · · · · · · · · ·

*T*he Church is something that should be loved, cherished,
celebrated, and valued by all Christians. The reality is that
many of us have had experiences with the Church that are not worth
celebrating and that call for genuine repentance and forgiveness,
which can be difficult to muster. When something is designed to be
beautiful and good, the perversion of what it should be is especially
saddening and hurtful. Even if we have not had a traumatic experience of abuse in the Church, many of us have experienced a gradual
and perhaps unintentional devaluing of the Church by allowing
spiritual habits to fall out of practice.

God forms the Church with beauty, design, and purpose. Your
place within the Body of Christ should provide you with comfort,
assurance, and security. The Church is a gift that Jesus has given
to each of us, through each of us. The Church is where Jesus gives
us His gifts of forgiveness and faith. Jesus gives the Church to you
and you to the Church.

Discussion Questions

1. What positive experiences have you had in the Church? When have you experienced the Church as the hands and feet of Jesus?

2. What negative experiences have you had in the Church? Rather than taking this opportunity to gossip, focus on why these experiences were especially hurtful. What good gift of our Savior was the Church supposed to offer in that moment? How did sin twist what should have been present?

3. Read 1 John 4:18–21. What does this passage teach us about our relationships with fellow Christians within the Church?

4. What can you do to be the Church? What is something you would like to focus on to grow in your understanding of the faith, your practice of the faith, or your proclamation of the hope that we have in Christ?

Lord of Creation, You tell us that the Church is sanctified not by anything we do but by the blood of Jesus. You promise to present the Church to Yourself without spot, wrinkle, or blemish. Forgive us for seeing the Church through our own eyes, for seeing the Church as something less than what You are making her to be. Teach us to love the Church as You do. Work through Your gifts of Word and Sacraments to give us comfort and assurance in Your love for us and in Your forgiveness. In Jesus' name we pray. Amen.

Leader Guide

Chapter 1:
The Origin of the Church

1. In Ephesians 5:22–33, Jesus is the one presenting His Bride, the Church, to Himself. He does it all—makes her clean, sanctifies her, and unites Himself to her. He lays down His life for her. In verses 29–31, Jesus sees the Church as part of Himself. He binds Himself to the Church, "and the two . . . become one flesh" (v. 31). Jesus views the Church as spotless, holy, and without blemish. He makes this reality by washing her with His blood.

2. Answers will vary. Do you find history dry? irrelevant? fascinating? intimidating? Consider and discuss why this might be. Learning about our history as the Church helps us draw comfort and strength from the many faithful witnesses that came before us. We also understand our own churches better when we know their backstory. When we know how and why the teachings and practices of our churches developed, we can better evaluate them according to Scripture and perceive which practices are truly helpful and which may lead us into error.

3. God's promises to Abraham find ultimate fulfillment in the Church. The Church is the "great multitude that no one could number, from every nation, from all tribes and peoples and languages" (Revelation 7:9), gathered around the throne of God. When Jesus returns and we live together forever in the new creation, we will finally be in the promised land to dwell in and possess.

4. Answers will vary.

Chapter 2:
The Rule of Faith

· · · · · · · · · · · · · · · ·

1. Answers for each passage are below.

- **2 Corinthians 6:14:** This verse demonstrates God's intolerance for falsehood. God is truth; therefore, we must not connect ourselves to those who speak against the truth. Picture two pack animals yoked together. If they are going in opposite directions, something will be torn apart and broken.

- **John 8:31–32:** Discipleship is about abiding in the Word of God. Other phrases to describe abiding in the Word are *resting in, marinating in, dwelling in, and immersing oneself in.* Our freedom comes from the Word of God, not from anything we do. Therefore, the most important part of what it means to be the Church is knowing His Word.

- **John 15:5:** We bear fruit when we are connected to Christ, the vine. From the previous passage and the surrounding context of John 15, we see that abiding in Christ means abiding in His Word. Galatians 5:22–23 describes the fruit that the Spirit works in us through the Word.

2. There are many different false teachers, and answers may vary. The first and most obvious indicator of a false teacher is if they make a statement that directly contradicts the plain meaning of Scripture or the creeds. Other things that might make you pause are if a teacher does not allow their words to be scrutinized against God's Word or if they

do not permit conversation or questioning. God's Word is not up for debate, but confidence that comes from the truth leads good teachers to be open to discussion and not defensive.

3. This text from 2 Peter teaches us that no doctrine or teaching of Scripture or of the Church has been produced by an individual. The writers of the Bible were inspired by the Holy Spirit. Therefore, the teachings of Scripture are from God, not from man. Beyond this, man does not have the ability to *interpret* Scripture in his own manner either. There is a correct interpretation, and it comes from God. We find that interpretation by immersing ourselves in the Bible itself, where the challenging passages are made clear by the straightforward passages. The more you study the Bible, the fewer confusing passages you will find. Scripture interprets Scripture.

4. The thing that makes us Jesus' disciples is abiding in His Word. Jesus says that those who "cannot bear to hear [His] word" are children of the devil. God's children hear God's Word, live in it, and believe it. Those who are not God's children hate God's Word. The comforting truth is that God works through His Word to strengthen our faith. We grow in our relationship with Him through His Word.

Chapter 3:
The Fellowship of the Saints

1. You can see the work of the Holy Spirit in the believers throughout each verse of this text. Living according to God's Word is always a response to the Holy Spirit working in our hearts. Verses 43 and 47 in particular showcase the Holy Spirit's work. In verse 43, the word *through* indicates that the works are not being done *by* the apostles but rather by the Holy Spirit working through their actions. Verse 47 reminds us that the growth of the Church is always the result of the Holy Spirit's work, not our own.

2. Answers will vary.

3. The Holy Spirit works through God's Word to bring us to faith and to sanctify us day by day. The Sacraments, where we receive forgiveness

of sins and strength to believe, are efficacious because of and through the spoken Word of God.

4. Romans 6:1–14 says we have been united with Jesus' death in our Baptism. Jesus died to free us from the grips of sin. By the power of the Holy Spirit, we should now live as if we are also dead to sin. Just as Jesus rose, we will one day rise. In the meantime, we still struggle with our sinful flesh and temptation, but we should strive to resist temptation and live according to God's good Law and design for us.

Chapter 4:
The Universal Church

. . . .

1. Answers may vary. Division in the Church is painful, often in very personal ways. It's okay to be honest about this. I think often for the sake of unity, we like to downplay how difficult division in the Church is for each of us, but this is rarely helpful for our interpersonal relationships or for our theological understanding.

2. Paul's description of the Church in this text is one of unity, selflessness, and care for others over one's selfish desires. He sets Jesus before us as the ultimate example of humility and service (see vv. 6–8). In verses 14–16, Paul exhorts readers to do all things without disputing so that their example may shine brightly in a world broken and tainted by sin. We do this by "holding fast to the word of life" (v. 16). In the light of divisions within the Church, this may seem paradoxical. How can we live at peace and yet hold fast to the truth when we disagree about what God's Word says? That is the challenging tension that we all face this side of eternity. The more we allow God's Word to shape and form our minds and hearts, the more we will become like Jesus, able to love others and bring peace to our relationships while continuing to hold to the truth.

3. Answers for each passage are below.

- **Romans 16:17–18:** In this verse, those who "create obstacles contrary to the doctrine that you have been taught" cause division (v. 17).

The concern is not chiefly about division but about the purity of the teaching, specifically that false teachers do not "create obstacles" by adding requirements for salvation to the Gospel, thus leading the faithful to stumble.

- **1 Corinthians 1:10:** We are to agree and "be united in the same mind and the same judgment." Here unity is regarding the doctrinal teachings of the Church, which must be agreed upon and held in common.

- **1 Corinthians 11:18–19:** Paul acknowledges that, this side of eternity, factions will exist, but they exist so that we may recognize those who are teaching the pure doctrine. If outward unity was more important than doctrinal purity, Paul would not have said this.

- **1 Corinthians 12:25:** All parts operate in unison in a healthy human body; there is no division. Likewise, in a healthy church, the Body of Christ is united and members care for one another.

- **Galatians 5:20:** Here "divisions" is listed alongside other "works of the flesh" (v. 19). Divisions in the Church result from our own sinful failings. We must live with division now because we are imperfect and cannot understand God's Word perfectly or love one another perfectly.

- **Titus 3:9–10:** Some things are foolish to quarrel about (v. 9). With this in mind, people who continue to stir up division after warnings should not be allowed to continue in their role in the Body of Christ. Paul advises Titus (who is a pastor) to cast them out.

- **Jude 19:** Those who cause divisions do not have the Holy Spirit. That is a serious accusation, but if a person appears to be causing division and yet is proclaiming the Gospel rightly, it is those who reject the Word who are truly responsible for division in God's eyes. Those who are faithful to the Word may be accused of sowing division, but this is not the case.

4. Answers will vary.

Chapter 5:
Authority and the
Pastoral Office

· · · · · · · · · · · ·

1. Titus 1:5–9 describes the ideal candidate for appointment as an overseer or elder (both of these terms are synonymous with *pastor*). A pastor is to be above reproach, meaning that he holds firmly to the Word of God and puts it into practice in his own life.

2. Answers will vary. Speaking from my own experience, pastors simply want their parishioners to come to church, come to Bible study, and make faithfulness to God a priority. They are encouraged when people physically show up to hear God's Word and receive the Sacraments. That's it! Gifts, invitations, and words of encouragement are indeed wonderful blessings for a pastor and his family, but at the end of the day, faithfulness to God's Word lived out and put into practice by weekly worship attendance is more encouraging and uplifting to a pastor than anything else.

   Pastors and their families often live far away from extended family, and this distance is compounded by not being able to travel for holidays like Christmas and Easter. Some ways you can support your pastor could be inviting him and his family over for a holiday dinner, offering free babysitting so he and his wife can go on a date, or offering handyman services if you know how to fix home appliances and the pastor does not have this skill set. Think about the way the congregation's demands may impact his family life and be willing to make adjustments if possible. If you are not sure what your pastor needs to feel cared for and joyful in his calling, ask him!

3. Answers will vary.

4. Answers will vary. Whenever someone is in a position to proclaim God's Word, they hold a position of power. If they proclaim words that are not from God and yet claim to speak with God's authority, this can be incredibly damaging and hurtful in countless different ways. Teaching false doctrine is spiritually abusive. Pastors teach by both their words

and their actions, which is why they are held to such a high standard of personal moral conduct.

5. Answers will vary.

Chapter 6:
Forgiveness and the Sacraments

1. Answers will vary. Chemnitz emphasizes that Jesus gives us the gift of Holy Communion to unite us to Himself, exchanging our sinful inadequacy for His righteousness. His body and blood, broken and shed for us, unite us to His death. By participating in Holy Communion, we are united with Christ in His atoning work. The cross is the source of our comfort, and in Communion, we can literally taste and feel our connection to that historic event on account of Christ. No wonder Chemnitz encourages us to receive the Lord's Supper often and with devotion!

2. The first half of this passage describes the Israelites and their struggle with idolatry and sexual immorality in the days following the exodus from Egypt. Paul emphasizes that while they all participated in the same spiritual food and drink (see vv. 3–4), not all of them were right before God. Some of them offered sacrifices to idols or indulged in sexual immorality and were struck down. Paul says that these accounts are written for our instruction so that we may guard ourselves against temptation as well. In verse 16, he speaks of Communion when he refers to "the cup of blessing that we bless." In Communion, we are made into one body with one another as we are united into Christ's Body. We should not participate in pagan practices (such as idolatry or sexual immorality) and also participate in the Lord's Supper. It is dangerous not only for our own souls but for the Body of Christ! We make a confession of unity and faith when we participate in the Lord's Supper; we should not think that this can be done flippantly, regardless of what other practices we also engage in.

3. Answers will vary.

4. Answers will vary.

Chapter 7:
Hope and the
Growth of the Church

· · · · · · · · · · · · · · · · · · · ·

1. Revelation 21 describes the new heaven and new earth coming down out of heaven. I find verses 3–4 particularly comforting. "The dwelling place of God is with man" (v. 3). All tears, death, mourning, and pain will pass away. When people experience pain and sorrow in this life, we have the privilege of reassuring them that Jesus cares deeply about that suffering. When He returns, He will make "all things new" (v. 5).

2. Answers will vary.

3. Answers will vary. Remember, even if we miss an opportunity to share God's comfort and truth with those who need it, it is the Holy Spirit who brings all people to knowledge of Christ. God does not need you. He can work through other people too. And there is forgiveness for "what we have left undone"[40] as well.

4. Answers will vary.

Chapter 8:
The Church for You

· · · · · · · · · · · · · · · · · · · ·

1. Answers will vary.

2. Answers will vary.

3. In 1 John 4, we read that it is impossible to love God while holding hatred in our hearts for a brother or sister in Christ. We have learned that we are united as the Body of Christ. You cannot profess to love Christ if there is a piece of Him that you hate. We are called in the Church to love one another as unconditionally as Jesus loves us. This does not

---

40   Divine Service Setting One, *LSB*, p. 151.

mean that our relationships in the Church will be perfect. We are all sinful, and sometimes our brother or sister will do things that are not commendable and are unloving. It is not truly love to allow someone to sin against us repeatedly, so sinful behavior must be called out and dealt with properly. But we are to be willing to forgive if and when our brother or sister in Christ repents. This is the kind of love that Jesus extends to each of us.

4. Answers will vary.

Acknowledgments

I would like to thank my husband, Jonathan, for always supporting me, for having countless conversations with me throughout this process, for encouraging me, and for reading everything I write before anyone else sees it. His love for me continues to remind me of Christ's love for the Church. Thank you also to my dear friends Deanna, Sarah, Rebekah, Kyle and Lis, and Nathan and Kendra for being my first readers and offering your thoughts and feedback. Your friendship and support are a tangible way that I find comfort through the Body of Christ. Thank you to the team at Concordia Publishing House for being a joy to work with and continually blessing the Church with resources faithful to God's Word. CPH is a blessing in every area of my life through the Bible studies, catechetical resources, and academic books they make available to God's people. It is an honor to be able to partner with them. And of course, thank you to my dear children for being patient with me as I make time to write. The Church is *for you*, and I pray you always find comfort in that truth.